The
REPUBLICAN
ROOSEVELT

The
REPUBLICAN
ROOSEVELT

By

JOHN MORTON BLUM

HARVARD UNIVERSITY PRESS
Cambridge, Massachusetts
1967

Distributed in Great Britain by
Oxford University Press, London
Fourth Printing

E
757
B65

85805

Library of Congress Catalog Card Number 54–5182
Printed in the United States of America

For PAMELA
Whose Dedications Are More Important

PREFACE

Since this is intended to be neither a biography of Roosevelt nor a complete record of his public career, but an interpretation of the purposes and methods of that career, I have elected to consider only what seems to me to be characteristic or revealing. Because Roosevelt was not a simple man, neither the selection nor the evaluation will satisfy everyone. The essay evolved, initially, to satisfy me. Like the others in the group editing *The Letters of Theodore Roosevelt*, I needed to fashion some chart to guide me through the processes of research and annotation. The chart grew slowly, taking its final form only as the work neared completion. It was fashioned, furthermore, collectively. The firmest lines belong to the whole group that edited. To an extraordinary degree, therefore, I am indebted to my colleagues, in particular to two of them: Alfred D. Chandler, Jr., taught us all much about American economic history and about business and governmental institutions; Elting E. Morison, the editor-in-chief, was a limitless source of our corporate inspiration. His unerring assessments of men and situations, his tolerance of our ways and his improvements on their fruits, not only gave shape to the eight volumes of letters but also gave to each of us an education in the writing of history, insight into the personality of Roosevelt, and an experience in happy human relations vastly more valuable than anything we produced.

To a number of other patient friends I owe a pleasant debt. Oscar Handlin, Richard W. Leopold, Frederick Merk, and Richard C. Overton by their perceptive criticism improved parts of the manuscript they generously read. Freely advancing their ideas in many conversations, these men and Duncan S. Ballantine, Kingman Brewster, Jr., and Frank B. Freidel helped me form and test my own. Eleanor G. Pearre gave her knowing attention to checking the accuracy and enhancing the form of the entire manuscript. For any errors in prose or fact or judgment that remain, I alone am responsible.

The data on which this book is based and the quotations it contains are taken almost exclusively from *The Works of Theodore Roosevelt*, National Edition, 20 vols. (New York, 1926), Charles Scribner's Sons; and *The Letters of Theodore Roosevelt*, 8 vols. (Cambridge, 1951–1954), Harvard University Press. *The Letters* perpetuated the errors in Roosevelt's holographs in order to reveal his dismal spelling. For the sake of clarity these errors have here been corrected. For permission to quote from *The Works* and *The Letters* I am indebted respectively to Scribner's and to the President and Fellows of Harvard College. The latter have also kindly consented to let me republish parts of essays which appeared as appendixes to Volumes II, IV, and VI of *The Letters*. For permission to quote from Lionel Trilling, *The Liberal Imagination* (New York, 1950), I am grateful to the Viking Press. In an appendix to the eighth volume of *The Letters* I have discussed the primary sources and some secondary sources on which this book, like *The Letters*, is based. The notes in *The Letters*, furthermore, list other secondary sources, many indispensable for information on or interpretations of Roosevelt.

1954   John M. Blum

PREFACE, 1962

In the years since this book was first published, American historians have substantially enlarged previous learning about Theodore Roosevelt and his times. Some of their additions and amendments bear upon interpretations in this volume, but, perhaps because questions of interpretation remain partly subjective, I have not much changed the views I held about Roosevelt in 1954. I have, however, concluded that I dismissed too lightly Roosevelt's claim to have presented a warning to the Kaiser during the controversy over Venezuela. On that matter, I find persuasive the account in the late Howard K. Beale's *Theodore Roosevelt and the Rise of America to World Power* (Baltimore, 1956). I have also claimed, I now believe, rather too much for Roosevelt and allowed too little to his associates in politics in my discussion of his relationship with James S. Clarkson during the months preceding the Republican convention of 1904. That issue has gained illumination from Leland L. Sage in his careful biography, *William Boyd Allison: A Study in Practical Politics* (Iowa City, 1956). Those two modifications strike me as significant for any study that, like this one, concerns itself with Roosevelt's understanding and use of power.

Rather more significant are three larger and more elusive problems. First, I believe I erred in failing to include in this book a full chapter about Roosevelt as an administrator, as Arthur S. Link has suggested in conversation I should have. Such a chapter would have revealed better than do those that follow how systematically Roosevelt sought and heeded the advice of intellectuals, experts on the various issues of his concern. More important, he recognized himself how large a part of governing administration was, and he brought to that function his always impressive energy and control. Second, I have profited since I first wrote from the astute suggestions of Richard Hofstadter in his *The Age of Reform* (New York, 1955), particularly his comments about Roosevelt's anxiety to bolster his own status and that of other men of his background. Certainly that anxiety contributed to the complex of motivations underlying his conduct. Last, and most difficult, there is the question of whether Roosevelt was in fact a conservative.

The definition of "conservative" ventured in Chapter I of this book is arbitrary, as Eric Goldman noted in a review, and therefore, as he also implied, without specific reference to the range of political attitudes prevalent in the United States of Roosevelt's time. Indeed the ingredients of that definition apply fully to many men who considered themselves "progressive," and who have been so considered by historians. For that reason and others, George E. Mowry in his *The Era of Theodore Roosevelt* (New York, 1958) — the most learned and thoughtful general account of the period — found Roosevelt a progressive, and in a review of that book I commended that finding. If historians can agree about what Roosevelt stood for, the label for his stance is not, I think, a matter of moment. Obviously they do agree, without important exceptions, that he was not a "liberal" in the sense of that adjective in his own day or earlier. And it was partly in contradistinction to "liberal" that I called him "conservative." But Professors Goldman and Mowry are right: Roosevelt was not one of the conventional conservatives of his day, and he was one, I think the most compelling one, of the American progressives.

Still, were it possible, as for this edition it is not, to rewrite Chapter I, I would not eliminate the discussion of Roosevelt as a conservative. Rather, I would expand upon it, for I think that progressivism was itself often conservative, within the meaning — however arbitrary — that I have attached to the latter word. Those progressives who shared Roosevelt's views were, it seems to me, seeking ways to accommodate American social, political, and economic institutions to advancing industrialism, with all that it implied. They were not seeking to uproot those institutions. They were seeking ways, too, to improve, but not to abolish, the processes by which a free society made decisions about governing itself and dealing with the rest of the world. And they were sensitive to the obligations of noblesse at home and abroad. They retained a faith in an old, but by no means quaint, morality. They renewed and refurbished another old faith, by no means irrelevant, in rationality, which they sometimes called science. They were, as it happens, not very different in their anxieties and their backgrounds from standpat Republicans (as the unpublished dissertation of Norman Wilensky reveals). But they were different in their public philosophy, and that difference, I believe, while one attribute of progressivism, was also a vital characteristic of a responsible, adaptable conservatism that has meaning still for American society.

But it is not the label, it is Roosevelt, that matters. As in 1954, so now, I am convinced that Theodore Roosevelt brought to public life qualities of person, a mastery of affairs, and a sense of the connectedness of the processes and the purposes of governing men that made him the most remarkable American of his generation, that made him also, at his best, an exemplar for American statesmen and their constituents in this century.

John Morton Blum
New Haven, 1962

CONTENTS

The
REPUBLICAN
ROOSEVELT

Chapter I

THE REPUBLICAN ROOSEVELT

So much of Theodore Roosevelt is comfortably familiar. There are the teeth, the famous intensity, the nervous grimace, impelling leadership, physical courage, moral fervor — sometimes frenzy. There is the falsetto exhorting the troops at the base of the San Juan ridge: "Gentlemen, the Almighty God and the Just Cause are with you. Gentlemen, CHARGE!" They did, of course, and they conquered. There are the busted trusts, the outdoor life, the nature fakirs, simplified spelling, rivers discovered, lions felled. There is the host of Armageddon dividing the Republican Party with revivalist abandon. Like pages out of G. A. Henty — vivid, seemingly ingenuous. But Henty is now little reopened, and Roosevelt is more often remembered than reread.

This is regrettable. Roosevelt's recently published letters, like his long-available public papers, reveal a broadly roaming and occasionally penetrating intelligence, an incomparable energy, a vastly entertaining and remarkably knowledgeable Republican politician. Whether or not he was a great man is unimportant. It is enough that the contributions he made to American life, particularly public life, and the ways in which he made them were often magnificent.

Because in mid-century the spirit of Roosevelt's time has become foreign, the man appears often in caricature. He should be seen against the background of the confidence he shared and fed — the belief that hard work was in itself a good thing, that whatever this hard work did was right; the conviction that the world had since the beginning of time progressed, so that men lived in the best of all possible worlds. From Roosevelt the laborers in this vineyard drew inspiration, for he showed them new tasks for active hands. This, Stuart Sherman, that clement critic of the age of confidence, understood. Disapproving as he did of many of Roosevelt's policies, he nevertheless admired the vitality whose example more than that of any other man led from the brokerages a generation of watchers in the woods and at the polls.

With Roosevelt, it is true, this generation embarked again and again on crusades of relative insignificance or of dubious merit. But they embarked. Again and again Roosevelt himself achieved triumphs which, however brilliant at the moment, afforded only ephemeral gain. But he achieved. Much in his career seems in retrospect scarcely worth the strong emotions and heated righteousness with which his speeches and letters were filled. But even when his just causes were narrowly partisan, he felt strongly. Today's insouciant critics, unlike Sherman, censure as quixotic adolescence or dangerous diversion the intensity of act and feeling they no longer share. Even they, however, do not find it dull.

Nor need they find it empty. Misplaced it sometimes was, and more often unimportant. But something beside remains. The war with Spain, for one thing, Roosevelt's finest hour, for all its unhappy aspects was a momentous affair. It was for him a device by which the United States assumed, at last, its proper place as a responsible world power. If he swaggered too much, he also foresaw, welcomed, and later developed the nation's role in maintaining international stability and promoting international justice. Concomitantly he championed not only military and naval preparedness but also the physical development of the country and the moral development of its people which constituted the resources for national greatness. And this also he did with confidence and by example. Before the coming of two wars, he hastened to volunteer. This was not sheer bellicosity. Roosevelt looked upon military service as he looked upon public service —

as the proper obligation of citizenship. The office did not have to seek the man.

If his just causes were sometimes not so just, his felt need so to define them was healthy. He had witnessed in his lifetime, as Americans only recently again have witnessed, the bankruptcy of public policy produced by callous disregard of morality. Honesty, he knew, was always an issue. Corrupt officials, like cruel forces of occupation, he found intolerable. Unlike most of the college bred of his generation, he did not choose to immunize himself. Mastering the tactics of the enemy, infiltrating their lines, in time occupying their strongholds, he ruled according to improved standards the domains they had held. As his motion was forceful, so his standards were high. In that combination Roosevelt had faith. By positive government he sought to promote national strength and to assure to each individual unfettered opportunity for realizing the dignity and the satisfactions of honest work. Whatever his shortcomings, his habit of action had enduring value. He made a virtue of dutiful vitality applied in an age of vigor and confidence. In a more troubled time the world learns painfully again the need for deciding firmly what is right and laboring assiduously to achieve it.

Roosevelt labored by his own choice as a politician. His decision to do so took courage, for his choice, when he made it, was disreputable. If he was, perhaps, called to politics by a craving for power, he needed nevertheless not only courage but also stamina to discipline that craving, to manage himself so that he could earn the chance to manage other men. This demanded what he called character, a splendid word which he never fully defined but never hesitated to use. Selecting a profession that satisfied his temperament, pursuing it with fortitude, he brought to it increasingly a perceptive practicability about the ways of gaining and utilizing high public office. Durable and sinewy were the roots of his career.

They had to be, for the roots of his convictions were also

tough. From his patrician family, from his high-Victorian God, from Harvard, for which he had always a tender regard, from nature — raw on western ranges or intellectualized in evolutionist tracts — from novels of romance and novels of realism, from history he read and history he wrote, he abstracted early in life principles of behavior which he honored to his death. He did not always abide by them. No politician could have. But he did attempt to abide, refusing either to abandon what he considered right or to let that consideration immobilize him. To his generation, as he would himself have said, he proved his truth by his endeavor.

He also demonstrated in a timeless way how Presidents succeed. The organization of his party, he knew, would determine his future; within the party, furthermore, the large decisions about the direction of public policy had to be made. A brilliant leader, he dominated his party, strengthening it as he worked. At the same time, if he did not dominate his constituents, he at least excited them and by pressure and persuasion won most of them to vote his way. So also with Congress. By negotiation, adjustment, discipline, and daring, he arranged that the laws he wanted most were passed. Because these operations took shape over long periods, only intimate examination of Roosevelt's professional performance reveals the joy and rigor in his relations, at once intuitive and controlled, with party, people, and Congress. Here was a rival for Mark Hanna, William Jennings Bryan, Nelson Aldrich; here a President who by tactics still significant resolved the persistent problems of his office; here a master among men who make things political work, make hustings howl with pleasure, conventions bow, and caucuses concede. Apart from anything Roosevelt attained, this virtuosity compels attention.

Roosevelt's proficiency in the processes of politics, administration, and legislation stamped him as a professional. Resting as it did on his unprotesting acceptance of established and relatively rigid political structures, this proficiency along with other qualities of mind and manner also suggested his affinity to latter-day conservatism. To be sure, Roosevelt was not a simple apologist for that familiar American conservative libation composed in equal parts of Herbert Spencer, Horatio Alger, and a protective tariff. Yet liberal historians — among many others Vernon Parrington, Henry Pringle, Arthur Schlesinger, Jr., and Daniel Aaron — have quite justly cashiered him from their serried champions of embattled workingmen and farmers. He was never a Jeffersonian. This helps to place him. Furthermore, although there was not in Roosevelt's life the stuff of a systematic philosophy of conservatism, in this country, in this century, perhaps, such a philosophy has not been systematic; certainly it has emanated from no one man, no Burke or Alexander Hamilton. And in Roosevelt's purposes and practices there appeared some attributes by and large common among those of his contemporaries whom liberals judged conservative.

These attributes can be enumerated. His preoccupation with the processes rather than the ends of government suggested that he considered democracy primarily a way of living. Valuing the institutions, forged in history, that mapped and stabilized this way, he endeavored to preserve them. But preservation, he realized, depended upon change. "The only true conservative," he told a fellow Progressive, "is the man who resolutely sets his face toward the future." So he believed in change, but gradual change; change within established institutions; change obtained by adapting, managing, administering; change "on suspicion." This was not political science but engineering, development by cut and test. There were requisites and rules for this development. It had to be directed from a position of power by men who appreciated what was and what had been. They had to be informed and, much more difficult, to be moral. Their information they could best obtain from successful operators in the field, ordinarily in Roosevelt's day businessmen, lawyers and financiers of parts and prescience. Their morality had primarily to come from character, ordinarily in Roosevelt's view a product of generations of good breeding or long seasons of hard work.

An institutionalist, a gradualist, a moralist, from the position he attained he ruled strongly and quite well. Learning the while, he developed large plans for the uses of power. These had one common, revealing objective: stability. The exercise of power at home, the concerts of power the world over, were intended first of all to provide order. If this was essential, it was not enough, for Roosevelt more and more identified the dimensions of stability with the man who drew them.

Furthermore, power was as ever an inadequate judge of its own virtue and, out of power, Roosevelt a fractious judge of those who had it. Lacking, as he did, a systematic sense of governmental ends, particularly when out of office he allowed his ambition to corrupt his methods. He was in opposition always carping, sometimes conscienceless. Ultimately, morality and information failed to restrain him. For this as much as any other reason the liberals cashiered him.

Often lamentably wrong, now and then possibly dangerous, Roosevelt nevertheless commands attention now just as he did while he lived. He was, after all, man acting, and as such he made mistakes. But from him something about conservatism may be learned, rather more about the ways of American political life, and a great deal both engaging and pertinent about the vigorous and the resilient applied boldly to that life. Besides all this, there was for those who knew him, there may be again for those who read of him, and there is still endlessly for those who write of him "the fun of him." For this, when he is finally weighed, he is found not wanting.

Chapter II

ROOTS OF CAREER

Theodore Roosevelt was a professional Republican politician from New York. He made a career of seeking and holding public office. His professional concern was with politics and government, with parties, elections, legislation, and rule. These simple, central facts in Roosevelt's life have been ignored, almost forgotten, in the thirty-odd years since his death. The builders and destroyers of a Roosevelt legend have demonstrated to their own satisfaction that he was either a great man or a perpetual adolescent, a champion of reform or a traitor to progressivism. The historians of naval policy, foreign policy, conservation and trust control have taken each a part of him and placed it in their chronicles. Too little, however, has Roosevelt been examined against the background of the institutions in which he deliberately chose to excel. Harvey Cushing without a scalpel, John Marshall without a robe, Stonewall Jackson without an army make no more sense than Theodore Roosevelt without a public office in hand or on order.

Perhaps the most extraordinary thing about Roosevelt's variegated, controversial personality was his choice of career. Well-bred, wealthy young men of old families simply did not, in 1880, choose to make a life's work of politics. It was common enough then for Harvard graduates of means and position to lend their extracurricular energies to a movement for civil service reform or to electing a cleanup ticket in Manhattan. It was appropriate for such men to write bitter books, which their friends read avidly, on the bankruptcy of public life. But it was unthinkable for them to abjure a study or a countinghouse for a continuing, intimate experience in the precincts of poverty or among the cuspidors of garish hotels where the cigar-smoking, whisky-drinking, evil old men of the parties then made their dull deals. The young Roosevelt shared the prejudices of his background. He later explained that he entered politics only because he wanted to bring to public life disinterested honesty of purpose. To some degree this was doubtless true. The sponsors of Roosevelt's first campaign for the New York Assembly probably expected from him only a term or two of legislative integrity. He ran in 1881 with reservations. "Don't think I am going to go into politics after this year," he predicted with gross inaccuracy, "for I am not." He found his first taste of politics "stupid and monotonous," most of his first colleagues "vicious, stupid looking scoundrels with apparently not a redeeming trait," or "well-meaning but very weak," or "smooth oily, plausible and tricky." He might still have made a career of the books he wrote in his giddy leisure; he might still have found a haven in publishing or a law office; he might even have disciplined his temperament to a life academic. Instead he quickly sought the speakership of the Assembly he almost despised, within three years put party regularity above public morality, within five years ran for mayor of New York City. Roosevelt made a career of politics, studied and mastered politics, because Roosevelt loved power.

Power is the business of partisan politics. Although only rarely divided on clear-cut issues, the major American parties have almost never, even in time of national peril, been willing to surrender political advantage for the sake of principle. For politicians, the unceasing quest for office, and with it power, is a first mark of professionalism. Yet, inhibited by their culture, Americans of polite society, while they freely select and acknowledge artistry, wealth, charity, the inculcation of learning or the advance of science as legitimate professional objectives, rarely dare to confess that their professional motive is political power. Particularly in the years of political degradation following the Civil War, such a confession could have elicited a response com-

parable only to a parental discovery of little boys reading indecent books behind closed doors. Consequently Roosevelt was
not candid. Until he intended, in 1908, to retire, he contended
to his own satisfaction that his motives were altruistic. He really
did "want . . . cautiously to feel . . . [his] way" to see if he
could not "make the general conditions of life a little easier, a
little better." He explained that he could accomplish this only
by adjusting to the system that provided the power to act. Even
when he brought himself to write more freely of power, he did
not acknowledge its importance for him as an end as well as a
means. This diagnosis convinced his friends, but it never fooled
the more discerning politicians who knew him and understood
him as one of themselves.

Roosevelt became a Republican without hesitation. The prejudices of birth and inheritance directed him to the party that
had in his childhood saved the union and that included during
his youth his father and his father's friends. For a moralistic
young man in Manhattan, furthermore, the Democracy offered
little. Bad as the Republican organization was, Tammany, by
reputation, was worse. In 1881 Boss Tweed was still a sharp
memory and the destitute, ignorant constituency upon which
Tweedism relied for votes was a depressing reality. Only slowly
did Roosevelt come to understand the important social services
the Hall rendered in return for support at the polls. At first, like
others who briefly sampled them, he found in the Democratic
machines of New York only callous, irremediable corruption
made less palatable by its association with a national party of
rebels, tradespeople, and immigrants. Observing the state Assembly at work, he confirmed his prejudices in his diary: "The
average democrat here seems much below the average Republican. Among the professions represented in the two parties the
contrast is striking. There are six liquor sellers, two bricklayers,
a butcher, a tobacconist, a pawnbroker, a compositor and a type-
setter in the house — all democratic; but of the farmers and
lawyers, the majority are Republican . . . even if the worst

elements of all, the twenty low Irishmen, were subtracted, the Republican average would still be higher than the Democratic."

Roosevelt's political persuasion, initially characteristic of his social associates, did not long continue to be so characteristic. For years New York men of family, while remaining faithful to the party of Lincoln, had combatted its new masters. While Roosevelt was at Harvard, his father clashed directly with President Grant's stalwart, corrupt agent in New York over the administration of the customhouse. By 1884 one national personification of Republican graft and patronage-mongering was the suave, deft senator from Maine, James G. Blaine, who in his long career adhered to no firm principle except his personal advantage. Roosevelt with his original friends and sponsors joined the fierce and futile battle to prevent the nomination of Blaine. "I will not stay in public life unless I can do so on my own terms," Roosevelt declared while he fought; "and my ideal . . . is rather a high one." He fought well at the state and national conventions but Blaine controlled the latter. Independent Republicans, at last rebellious, in large numbers left the party, declaring for Grover Cleveland, the Democratic candidate. Roosevelt hesitated. He then declared for Blaine.

A member of the Assembly while Cleveland was Governor of New York, Roosevelt knew very well that the Democrat was an honest, courageous man. Cleveland had, of course, made the usual arrangements with local leaders whose friendship he, like any governor, needed. At times these arrangements had directly crossed Roosevelt's purpose. Yet the governor, by the standards of personal integrity and political decency, was incontestably preferable to Blaine. These standards Roosevelt claimed as his own. He understood that in 1884 they particularly needed the rigorous championship they deserved. But alienating old friends, straining his own conscience, Roosevelt stumped for Blaine, "of all the men presented to the [Republican] convention . . . by far the most objectionable." "It is impossible for me to say," he admitted, "that I consider Blaine and Logan as fit nominees."

"Yet beyond a doubt . . . ," he had to confess, Blaine "was the free choice of the great majority of the Republican voters of the northern states." And as between Blaine and a Democrat, Roosevelt did not hesitate long. Following the advice he gave to his Massachusetts friend, Henry Cabot Lodge, he kept on good terms with the machine "and put in every ounce, to win." Accepting, as he did, the verdict of the party, the method by which it had been reached, and the strength of the men who engineered it, Roosevelt declared not only for Blaine but also for professionalism. In time, he might have reasoned, his own turn would come.

Roosevelt suffered for this decision. Self-appointed keepers of the patrician conscience, many of whom he had admired, damned him for it. Roosevelt resented their assaults, the more because he knew the justice of their cause. A combative man, for like reasons he returned their vituperation in kind. During Blaine's campaign he managed, with Lodge, to picture Cleveland as rather worse than the whole Grant gang. During most of the rest of his life, partly because he envied the moral freedom of political independence, he attacked his detractors bitterly. But if Roosevelt felt the need to defend himself, he had few doubts about the logic of his decision. As much as ambition, a nice recognition of the conditions of political life moved him to professionalism. Independence was too expensive a pleasure. Rightly or wrongly, the two-party system was established. Dissent within a party was one thing; bolting quite another. From 1884 on Roosevelt for good reason insisted that a "healthy party spirit" was "prerequisite to the performance of effective work in American political life."

Later experience sustained Roosevelt's observation. In municipal elections, where party lines were less sacred and less meaningful than in national affairs, he ventured occasionally to support independent tickets. But their repeated failures, he quickly learned, by splitting the Republican vote helped Tammany control the city. In Albany and Washington the opposition of single-minded reformers to party compromises essential for a majority vote prevented or delayed legislation which would have accomplished a part at least of their purpose. More and more, therefore, Roosevelt struggled "'mighty hard' to stay in the Republican party." When, in 1896, the Democracy absorbed populism and through William Jennings Bryan gave it a silver cadence, Roosevelt found his party a precious fortress of stability. The prejudices of his youth, though softened; the habit of sixteen years, then hardening; the fear of radical change combined to reinforce his regularity. The "crooks" and the "criminals," the anarchists and the socialists, "organized labor in the lowest unions" and "the slow, obstinate farmer" now comprised his opposition. It had to be defeated.

Yet Roosevelt's was regularity with a conscience. "Public men," he mused, "have great temptations. They are always obliged to compromise in order to do anything at all." Practical but restless, he drew a shaky line between partisanship and "offensive partisanship." He would not bolt, but within the party, or in office on party sufferance, he attempted to further his own ideas as well as his own career. He retained "a feeling of profound anger and contempt alike for the malicious impracticable visionary . . . and for the vicious and cynical professional politicians." The "visionary reformers," Roosevelt admitted, provided a "vital spark which must be breathed into the machine." While they sparked, he would breathe it in. While they chafed, he would labor, as he so constantly repeated, for realizable ideals.

During Roosevelt's first campaign for the Assembly, Joe Murray, an Irish Republican ward heeler, explained the division of labor: let the candidate attend to platform, perorations, and petitions for patrician support; unembarrassed by his presence Murray would in his own manner muster the habitués of the corner saloons. Later, with more experience, Roosevelt could bear an occasional hand on the street corners. Even then his foremen claimed their role and their rewards. For Murray, whose good luck in picking a winner permitted him to reach offices beyond the limits of his capacity, Roosevelt retained a lifelong affection born of gratitude and tempered with caution. He appointed Murray periodically to positions of more income than responsibility, each time admonishing him to behave. Anything less would have violated the law of loyalty in politics; anything more would have abandoned the public welfare to beguiling incompetency.

A personal staff, Roosevelt early discovered, however efficient, was inadequate. Blaine prevailed at the convention of 1884 because his managers had negotiated alliances with other regional leaders. Roosevelt in 1888 assisted in making similar, successful arrangements for Benjamin Harrison, the Republican nominee. Even within a municipality a politician could not go it alone. This Roosevelt learned painfully. Although overshadowed by his adventures in the Bad Lands, his political career between the national conventions continued unabated. In 1886, after wiser men had refused, he accepted the Republican nomination for mayor of New York. Against him there stood both Henry George, prophet of radicalism in his day, choice of organized labor, and Abram S. Hewitt, pillar of respectable Democracy, choice of Tammany Hall. Roosevelt made a spirited canvass emphasizing the need for morality in municipal government, which Tammany, he argued, could not supply, and denying the existence of a class issue, which George sought to exploit. In spite of his youth and his formidable opposition, he ran a strong third. As he later observed, he might have won had not the Republicans scratched the ticket to vote for Hewitt. Many did so because their fear of George overcame their antipathy to Tammany. Many others followed the dictates of Republican leaders who traded votes to Tammany in return for promises of patronage. After 1886, Roosevelt did not again enter the lists without first carefully checking the intentions of his supporting entente.

Roosevelt received his most thorough indoctrination in the devices of political organization by opposing them. Recognizing as he did the need for organization and regularity, he nevertheless, while Civil Service Commissioner, warred on the system without which his party had never functioned. In his six years in office he courageously advanced the application and the popularity of the merit system. For its sake Roosevelt clashed not only with the designing Democratic rotators of office who accompanied Grover Cleveland on his return to the White House in 1893, but earlier, more boldly, with the Republicans who from 1889 to 1893 impounded patronage for Harrison. Along with the preëminent protagonists of civil service reform, Roosevelt fought the wholesale removals made by the spoilsmen of Harrison's administration, particularly Assistant Postmaster General James S. Clarkson. But even as he battled for the right, perhaps unconsciously he absorbed their lore.

Harrison's renomination, threatened by the reviving ambitions of Blaine, owed much to Clarkson. The Assistant Postmaster General skillfully disposed of bounties to shock troops in Indiana, the President's native state; to the district lieutenants of such powerful state leaders as Senator Matthew Quay of Pennsylvania; particularly to the manageable masters of the masquerade that is the Republican party in the South. Harrison's campaign for reëlection, although unsuccessful, gained strength from Clarkson's operations in such doubtful states as Maryland where the precarious balance of party power enhanced the importance of political favors, large or small. As he resisted Clarkson's maneuvers, as he attempted to extend the merit system and thereby delimit the area of potential patronage manipulation, Roosevelt dealt intimately with the power flows of politics. The experience impressed him.

Yet for a while still the young man struggled. Even for an ambitious patrician, it was not easy to believe that government belonged no longer to the talented and well-bred, to learn that perhaps it never had, to confess that the quest for power, if it did not corrupt, at least at times demoralized. It was disconcerting to discover that the Five of Hearts was never trump. It was uncomfortable to make of party regularity, balanced tickets, personal alliances and political rewards a position of strength. Briefly, as police commissioner under an independent mayor of New York, Roosevelt — not without hedging, always locally — resisted much of what he already knew he had to accept. Soon seeking release, he appealed almost abjectly to Republican stalwarts for appointment as Assistant Secretary of the Navy. They complied. For sixteen years he did not turn again.

By 1898, when he ran for Governor of New York, Roosevelt had taken firmly his position of strength. Senator Thomas Collier Platt, the "easy boss" of New York Republicans, accepted Roosevelt, about whom he was "a mite apprehensive," only because he needed a candidate with the glamor of the hero of San Juan to curtain the disrepute of the Republican incumbent. But virtue alone had not brought reward. Platt would have rejected Roosevelt had not the Colonel guaranteed to play fair. Roosevelt's performance was accomplished. In his negotiations for the nomination, he rejected the overtures of the independents, some of them his personal friends. Certifying his party regularity, he promised he would "treat with and work with the organization," "see and consult the leaders — not once, but continuously — and earnestly try to come to an agreement on all important questions with them . . ." But, he warned, "when we come to . . . anything touching the Eighth Commandment and general decency, I could not allow any consideration of party to come in." This was good enough for Platt who also professed to believe in the Decalogue. It provided, he reckoned, the matter and cadence for first-rate campaign orations.

Roosevelt campaigned professionally. Either directly or through his field commanders he patronized the Irish and the Germans, the Jews and the Catholics, labor and capital. To a balanced ticket and a balanced program he added the enchantment which Platt knew the party needed. On the stump, as an old friend remarked, "Teddy . . . [was] a wonder . . . there were immense gatherings of enthusiastic people at every stopping place . . . [Even when] the speech was nothing, . . . the man's presence was everything. It was electrical, magnetic." The speeches said much of the glories of the recent, apparently Republican, war with Spain and a great deal more about the hideous evils of government by Tammany. This was a serviceable formula. Roosevelt won.

His larger test lay ahead. He had to keep his pledge to Platt — to reward, to consult; and yet — if his present were to be morally tolerable and his future bright — overcoming the reluctance of the organization that controlled his legislature, he had also to sponsor successfully substantial change. During his eleven years in Washington Roosevelt had daily watched three Presidents in a similar pass. Benjamin Harrison, cold, diffident, incapable of arousing a constituency, had let himself become a captive. Cleveland struggled, but during his second term his stubborn neglect now of the people, now of his party, offended alternately the hinterland and the Hill. William McKinley did better. Using, as had his predecessors, the pressures of patronage, he also relied upon the inscrutable Mark Hanna and his associates to make up the mind of the caucus as they seemed to poll it. From each of these, negatively or positively according to his abilities, Roosevelt drew the lessons to satisfy his needs.

Roosevelt took care that Platt and his lieutenants received an abundant crop of political plums, but diligently he graded this yield. From the deserving Republicans who sought appointive office, he selected consistently the limited best talents available for service in state posts. Platt, now and then irritated, only once became angry. In spite of the senator's insistence, Roosevelt refused to reappoint the incumbent Superintendent of Insurance, a "stench in the nostrils of the people" of New York. To mobilize public support, Roosevelt broadcast his rediscovery of that official's past indiscretions. Patiently he explained his intention to the leaders of the party. Wisely he selected for appointment a tried professional politician who was both acceptable to the organization and equipped for the job. The Senate accepted the governor's man — a less regular candidate could not have been confirmed.

With comparable calculation Roosevelt handled legislation. He attempted nothing for which there was no precedent. Informing Platt always of his plans, he adjusted many to meet the senator's objections, persuaded Platt often also to adjust, and judiciously abandoned most of what could not be compromised. Roosevelt was able to persuade the senator only because he would, Platt realized, at times proceed alone. These occasions were rare, but when they arose Roosevelt mastered them. He ventured rebellion only when he could be sure that a majority of the people and a substantial fraction of his party stood with him. To impel the enactment of a measure taxing public utilities franchises as real property — the signal statutory achievement of his administration — Roosevelt, facing down the organization, drew upon an aroused popular opinion, directed adroitly the operations of the Republican legislators assisting him, and at the moment of crisis interceded personally and dramatically. He would not be Platt's captive but, as he himself attested, he would not be Platt's foe. Keeping the essence of his promise, Roosevelt used the party as an instrument of action. This enhanced his reputation. It also protected, indeed strengthened, his implement. With comfortable pleasure Roosevelt described this "hodgepodge compounded of the ideal and the practicable" as "simply the combination which made Washington and Lincoln great powers for good."

But executive leadership, even in the tradition of the immortals, Roosevelt regarded as but one measure of executive success. "The bulk of government," he maintained, "is not legislation but administration . . ." He had always the qualities of personality essential for that unspectacular function. He enjoyed and valued hard work. He identified with the offices he held. He liked people and judged them with discernment. He sought and took advice. Temperamentally aggressive, impatient with the safety of inaction, he delighted in making decisions. All this made his indoctrination in administration — his tenure as Civil Service Commissioner, Police Commissioner, and Assistant Secretary of the Navy — as exasperating as it was thorough. The limitations of authority and information that confined the offices he held continually frustrated Roosevelt. The Civil Service Commission had to rely upon almost every other agency in the executive departments, over none of which it had any direct control, for a large proportion of its personnel and materiel. Inevitably its larder was bare. The three commissioners, selected in accordance with law on a bipartisan basis, made decisions by majority vote. Inevitably dissent arose, retarded action, and, bruited about on both ends of Pennsylvania Avenue, cost the agency prestige. The police commission, also bipartisan, consisted of four members who could act on certain matters only by unanimous vote, on others only by majority. The commission, furthermore, had less authority over some promotions than did the chief of police. The comptroller could hold up its funds; the mayor could vitiate its policies; the state government could legislate it out of existence. The situation in the Navy Department was only superficially better. Responsible officially only to the President, the Secretary of the Navy was in fact the captive of his bureau chiefs, the naval officers who administered the business departments of the service. While politicians came and went, the bureau chiefs remained, accumulating power in their separate bailiwicks and controlling the information without which no Secretary could function. To Roosevelt's efforts to abolish or to circumvent these obstacles, his superiors gave little encouragement. Often his advice to them on policy or on how to make policy was unreasonable, but more often, as he judged, it was wise. He chafed not only over defeat, not only because — like any confident, capable man — he wanted the satisfaction of self-direction, but also because he realized that efficient government depends upon the delegation of authority as well as of responsibility.

When his became the superior position, this realization became his policy. Although reorganization is perhaps the slowest, most resisted, least rewarding activity within the power of a chief executive, Roosevelt either directly or through his subordinates attempted to define and separate administrative functions and to define and pinpoint responsibility. As governor he improved the organization of the canal system, the state's corrective institutions, and the factory inspector's office. Given more time and a larger opportunity, as President he accomplished more in remodeling administrative structures than had all his predecessors since Lincoln. Roosevelt was often awkward, or at least unsystematic. He measured his bureaucracy not by neatness but by results. From one principle, however, he did not deviate: for responsible positions he sought out first-rate men. There were, of course, too few of these, particularly for state administration. When one could not be found, Roosevelt overrode his subordinates as his superiors had overridden him. But at all times avoiding cronyism, nepotism, and like malaise, he very rarely made a really bad appointment and he gave office to many able men. Never afraid of being overshadowed by their reputation or performance, he gave them independence and, when by law he could, authority. Because he offered them the possibility and therefore the satisfactions of achievement, he could recruit and retain subordinates of stature. This remains a bold and rare talent.

From his staff Roosevelt expected not only force but also information and advice. Its counsel he supplemented by soliciting the opinions of experts on every issue to which he adverted. A scrupulous administrator by the time Roosevelt entered public life could work no other way, for the problems of government had already become too intricate for the amateur. Only from specialists, rich in practical experience, had he been able to learn with precisely what conditions state housing legislation had to deal, by exactly what procedures the merit system functioned, by specifically what methods the navy procured and readied ships and men. In high office, Roosevelt turned by habit to the informed. The foremost American economists, lawyers, and union leaders at his request submitted knowledgeable briefs from which while governor he synthesized his programs for the regulation of corporations and the protection of labor. For counsel on railroad and canal transportation and on the reorganization of the government of New York City, he relied upon groups of experts appointed to investigatory commissions. Deliberately by consultation Roosevelt disciplined his use of the power he pursued.

This personal procedure Roosevelt ultimately generalized. The legislative process, susceptible as it was to regional and partisan influences, at best intermittent and inexpert, he always distrusted. In Washington and Albany political pressures distorted law. The vacillating Congresses of Harrison and Cleveland, backing and filling on tariff and monetary policy, produced fearful insecurities. Roosevelt's legislature in New York let local loyalties delay the dredging of the barge canal. The executive, unlike the legislature, could act continuously and directly, yet the executive was also politically vulnerable and often uninformed. To remove these liabilities and to channel the power to act, Roosevelt came more and more to advocate the use of administrative commissions, staffed by nonpartisan specialists, free from legislative interference. The Civil Service Commission, whatever its deficiencies, had, he knew, improved immeasurably the distribution of federal offices. Could each large question of government be defined in manageable dimensions and referred to administrative agencies, could these be properly organized, adequately empowered, and staffed by competent men of sure character, they could — he concluded — by continuing operations in a familiar situation control it. The power of such agencies he proposed to restrain not by checks and balances but as he restrained himself. Just as he divided his authority by delegating distinguishable parts of it to his subordinates, so would he divide the executive's assignable functions among its several agencies. More important, just as he disciplined his power by consultation, so would the personnel in any agency, uninhibited in its area of authority, be restrained by the logic of their accumulated information and experience.

Assessing his governorship, Roosevelt concluded that administration, "the bulk of government," "has been done on about as near an ideal basis as I can get it done." Indisputably his administration was impressive. To the structure and staff of the state he had given much of the rigor that he was more generously to contribute to their national counterparts. If he was when he left Albany perhaps too optimistic about the use of power, he was at least unafraid. He had learned, in any case, to organize and to control not only his staff but also — beyond that area where politics did it for him — himself. These were to be salutary assets, for the times, whatever else they needed, needed a bold manager, trained to manage.

❋

Enjoying as he did the power of the governorship, savoring the small dramas in which his was the leading role, Roosevelt hoped for renomination. Yet he yielded gracefully, when the time came, to the Republican chieftains, including Senator Platt, who thrust upon him in 1900 the nomination for Vice-President. Platt wanted him out of New York; others wanted him on the national ticket to tilt in the hinterlands with Bryan. Roosevelt was graceful in accepting perhaps largely because he knew he had to yield. But Roosevelt also had always an incurable case of Potomac fever. In facing the problems of New York State, moreover, in meeting there with new immediacy the issues then troubling the nation, he found evidence to confirm his long-growing conviction that, for the most part, only the federal government could cope successfully with the determining forces of American society. By 1900 he had thoughts of the Presidency which he dared not articulate. He intended from the first to make the Vice-Presidency a stepping stone. Opposing his nomination, Mark Hanna reportedly said in exasperation to Roosevelt's sponsors: "Don't you realize that there's only one life between this madman and the White House?"

In describing Roosevelt as a madman, Hanna erred. Ambitious Roosevelt was, but as a politician, not as a paranoiac. With no less discernment than Hanna himself, he understood his calling; with no less dexterity, he followed it. By 1900 Roosevelt's party regularity had become convincingly habitual; his utilization of the mechanics of power, as Platt could attest, smoothly effectual; his standards of executive efficiency, refreshingly rigorous. These were not the attributes of madness. Perhaps Hanna meant that Roosevelt was a radical. The radicals of 1900, however, agreed with Henry Demarest Lloyd, one of their number, that Roosevelt had no "ear" for their "new music of humanity." They knew him to be a conservative.

Hanna may have been confused because Roosevelt's was not the sterile conservatism of *laissez faire*. Entering politics as he did in order not only to reign but also to rule, Roosevelt never purposed that his role in government be exclusively that of an umpire. He was by personality incapable of believing that his best activity was his least activity. At the same time, he did not intend that a dogmatic body of convictions, whether of the left or of the right, should deny him the chance to reign and therefore the chance to rule. His profession molded him. To harness the clashing elements that made up his party, to court the conflicting interests upon which the success of campaigns and of proposed legislation depends, he learned continuously to compromise. To administer a general law or policy as it had to apply to specific situations, he learned continuously to adjust. Such adaptiveness can produce either selfish opportunism or purposeful pragmatism. A conscionable professional, Roosevelt was not a mere opportunist. He did not, like many of his liberal contemporaries, expect new laws or new theories in themselves to provide good government. To that end he relied upon his own strength of character, upon the agencies of administration he valued, and upon the able men he sought out for appointments. He concerned himself rather with processes and instruments than with finalities.

This was not a position that lent itself to definition. Even Roosevelt, at the peak of his career, could not be sure whether he was a "conservative radical" or a "radical conservative." He was sure, at least, that he believed in the gospel of good works. This was enough for him, but not for that critic who complained that Roosevelt had policies but never principles. Of policies, of course, he had scores; he also had principles, but largely principles of behavior. Perhaps by 1900 one basis of political conservatism was such an untheoretical creed, adaptive, concerned with the pursuit and use of power for the control of specific situations, depending upon able, informed and honest men disciplined only by their principles of behavior; ineffectual, perforce, in the hands of the weak, dangerous in the hands of the corrupt or of the unrestrained.

Toward such a conservatism Roosevelt's early career moved him. Politics temper the ideologies of ambitious men. Roosevelt admitted that convictions in politics were embarrassing. Yet he avoided callous opportunism. He tempered his pragmatism with sympathy and morality. He directed his power with expert information. And even as he absorbed, largely subconsciously, the meaning of his career, he developed consciously convictions that that career often challenged. The conflict hurt. The career almost always won. Yet the convictions provided Roosevelt with a purpose distinct from power itself and, more important, with a foundation for the indispensable principles by which he attempted, at least, to behave.

Chapter III

ROOTS OF CONVICTION

There was almost nothing that did not interest Theodore Roosevelt, almost nothing about which he would not or could not think. An energetic, versatile intelligence, he began early in life to turn his mind, even during his busiest seasons, to the broad complex of his world. He matured in an exciting time — the age, in America, of rapid industrialization, Darwinism, the beginnings of scientific scholarship and critical realism. Omnivorously curious, as student, author, and critic Roosevelt studied these separate but often related phenomena. Gradually he formed basic conclusions about nature, society, literature, and government. By the time he was elected to high office, these conclusions, in spite of their superficial disorganization, had become — within the inevitable limits of the politically practicable — the controlling principles of his career. Ambitious alike for himself and his country, Roosevelt well knew the awful perplexity of a man of convictions who felt compelled to realize them in action.

The earliest consuming interest of Roosevelt's boyhood was nature. Encouraged by his father, a director of the Museum of Natural History, he found favored playmates among mice, guinea pigs, chipmunks, and squirrels. Spectacles, a shotgun, and lessons in taxidermy introduced him to the world of birds. While hunting them and studying their habits, he read precociously what books he could find. Roosevelt's careful inspection of the coloring of Old World chats, made in his teens with the aid of an ornithological treatise, supplied evidence which he used years later to challenge a too-generalized theory of protective coloring. At college and in the Dakotas he continued to examine and record the life of birds and animals in their natural habitats. His intimate familiarity with the wapiti, cougar, and other creatures of the western plains and Long Island swamps, his sound inductive conclusions on the nature of species and subspecies, proved valuable to professional scientists.

Roosevelt's investigation of nature stopped short of the laboratory. Disliking confinement, he gloried in life in the wilds rather than in the science of the microscope and dissecting table. If Roosevelt would not be a biologist, he nevertheless followed scientific thought with eager understanding, some of it with "a devotion . . . usually attended by a dreary lack of reward." At Harvard he won "honorable mention" in natural sciences. And especially in reading Charles Darwin and Thomas Huxley — Darwin's friend, protagonist and popularizer — he found both delight and reward.

The influence of Darwinian thought on Roosevelt's generation was profound. Historians, sociologists, and economists transposed Darwin's theses on evolution to their disciplines, sometimes with caution and salutary effect, more often indiscriminately and with regrettable results. Following Herbert Spencer, they identified the conception of the survival of the fittest with divine purpose. Evolution, animal or social, was a progressive movement toward a better life. Its course was not to be altered or interrupted. Roosevelt, approaching Darwin with a nice appreciation of the subject, accepted evolution through struggle as an axiom in all his thinking. Life, for him, was strife. Individuals and societies progressed or retrogressed depending on their ability to fight and to adjust. But Roosevelt, a competent naturalist, comprehended the limitations of Darwin's hypotheses. He realized that Darwin's postulates, especially when transposed to human experience, needed documentation and refinement. Furthermore, he had no sense of divine purpose. For him the evolutionary process was secular and scientific. Roosevelt, therefore, tempered his Darwinism with inductive conclusions and nonbiological premises and prejudices.

"The progress of mankind in past ages," Roosevelt observed in 1895, "can only have been made under, and in accordance with, certain biological laws, and . . . these laws continue to work in human society at the present day . . . [They] govern the reproduction of mankind from generation to generation, precisely as they govern the reproduction of the lower animals, and . . . therefore, largely govern his progress." But he gave natural selection no monopoly in the determination of human progress. Eugenics, especially social eugenics, Roosevelt had learned, was a complicated process. To a degree selection was most rigid, he pointed out, where fecundity was greatest, but the species which had the greatest fecundity made the least progress: consider the fate of the guinea pig. There were, moreover, certain "curious features" in human society. Where the struggle for life was too intense, energy was dissipated in seeking bare existence, and national progress was inhibited. The English and German peoples had fared better than the Italians, Poles, and Irish. On the other hand, loss of fecundity was fatal. A declining population, witness the French, endangered a nation. Insofar as the biological analogy applied, progress in human society depended on the steady rise of the lower class to the level of the upper as the latter tended to vanish. This improvement, Roosevelt had earlier declared, was "due mainly to the transmission of acquired characters, a process which in every civilized State operates so strongly as to counterbalance the operation of that baleful law of natural selection which tells against the survival of the most desirable classes."

Agreeing that many of the plans proposed in the interest of oppressed individuals were destructive of social growth, Roosevelt would not reject all such plans. He denied the contention that scientific development showed the interests of the group and the individual to be antagonistic. On the contrary, Roosevelt argued, the individual had a rational interest in conduct subordinate to the welfare of society, for in the process of social evolution men had reached the stage where they felt "more shame and misery from neglect of duty, from cowardice or dishonesty" than could be offset by the gratification of individual desires. Character had kept pace with animal evolution, making the growth of rationalism, when accompanied by the growth of ethics and morality, the key to human progress. Intellect and morality, progressing together, Roosevelt declared, "will persistently war against the individuals in whom the spirit of selfishness . . . shows itself strongly." The development of intellect, while necessary, was less important than the development of character, for the "prime factor" in social evolution was the "power to attain a high degree of social efficiency." "Social efficiency," in turn, derived from "love of order, ability to fight well and breed well, capacity to subordinate the interests of the individual to the interests of the community, . . . and similar rather hum-drum qualities." Progress, Roosevelt had maintained in another context, might be assured "if we but live wise, brave, and upright lives," if each plays "his part, manfully, as a man among men."

These interpretations permitted Roosevelt to conclude that "the true function of the State, as it interferes in social life, should be to make the chances of competition more even, not to abolish them." Earlier Roosevelt had stated his belief that raising the standard of living for the mass of people did not necessarily mean lowering the standard of "the fortunate few." Contemplating communities of the future without extremes of poverty and wealth, he suggested that for such a development "the sphere of the State's action may be vastly increased without in any way diminishing the happiness of either the many or the few." State socialism was neither necessary nor probable, but Spencerian *laissez faire* was patently inadequate for the "greatest victories . . . yet to be won."

Roosevelt had no hesitation in maintaining that not all groups were equally endowed with the qualities prerequisite for social efficiency. The black and yellow peoples, he believed, were ignorant and unprogressive. While not excluding the possibility that they might improve their lot, he clearly relegated them to an inferior evolutionary status. He more often classified societies by nation than by color. Here the inferior "races" were the southern and eastern Europeans. Depressed conditions in those areas, he implied, evidenced a lack of potential in the national struggle for existence. Of the northern Europeans, the favored people, Roosevelt championed the Anglo-Americans. His *Winning of the West* suggests that the Anglo-Americans enjoyed a biological as well as a cultural supremacy. Within the United States he considered the "native American" communities most progressive. This strain of thought took political expression in the arguments for a literacy test, which Roosevelt endorsed.

Nevertheless, Roosevelt opposed intolerant nativism. His faith in Anglo-American institutions sustained his faith in the efficacy of the "melting pot." The immigrants of the slums he blamed in part for corrupt government, but he confidently expected that second- and third-generation Americans would overcome the weaknesses of their forebears as they learned from the American environment. Roosevelt, therefore, did not fear "the mass." The proletariat could be assisted by the state. And like the vulgar rich, they could improve themselves by following the example set by men "of good blood . . . meaning blood that had flowed through the veins of generations of self-restraint and courage and hard work, and careful training in mind and in the manly virtues." So long as the "melting pot" was not overcrowded, Americans of all origins, given time, would develop the character necessary for their own progress.

These attitudes were rooted in Roosevelt's childhood. From his father and his father's friends he received his introduction to the social gospel. Familiar from youth with the ethics of the Bible, he was even more familiar with their application in philanthropy and social work. The inequalities evidenced in the lives of the very poor impressed Roosevelt long before he became governor. Only with time did he modify the patrician noblesse of his father's ministrations to impecunious newsboys, but as Sunday school teacher, legislator, and Police Commissioner he daily observed that the race was not necessarily to the swift, for the swift too often were kept from the post. Roosevelt consequently rejected the attitude toward poverty of the Malthusians and social Darwinists. He was not, ordinarily, a compassionate man. Perhaps, however much he may have understood, he did not love mankind. But he was gregarious. In politics, at roundups, in battle, he worked and fought with all types of men and won their admiration. Very rarely, and then only reluctantly, did he appoint impoverished or unlettered men to responsible office. But he felt that they deserved better housing, shorter hours of labor, increased opportunities to reach a higher level of existence. In dealing with the poor, Roosevelt was never intimate, but neither was he satisfied with hymns and handouts as antidotes for destitution.

From his childhood Roosevelt also carried over the American bourgeois morality. In his world a heart of gold beat gently in each fair feminine breast, a leg was a limb, and sex a description of gender. Others, while concurring in those virtuous views of physical conduct, were peculiarly indifferent to social morality. But not Roosevelt. He believed in the gospel of work. He also believed that the Eighth and Ninth Commandments should restrain the pursuit of success. In part because he had no need to defend a newly acquired fortune or to excuse a suspicious political past, Roosevelt established for himself a stern moral code by which he rejected the amorality of business and public as well as of private life. Too much a political realist to refuse to coöperate with businessmen and politicians, he was, nevertheless, neither personally dishonest nor given to compromise where opinion was unfettered by political considerations. When expounding theory, he aggressively asserted that the struggle for existence in human society was subject to rules of behavior inapplicable to other species.

Roosevelt approached literature with these moral criteria. Like most men, he enjoyed a good story, and like most of his contemporaries, he favored romanticism in belles-lettres. But his primary requirements were that a novel demonstrate the validity of his rules of behavior and do so in genteel language. Roosevelt made no allowance for the spirit or the vocabulary of other times. Chaucer, he felt, was "altogether needlessly filthy." Plot was even more important than vocabulary. If a heroine were to be shot, she should be wounded, not killed. It was not proper to kill women, even fictional women. It was equally improper to seduce them or to be seduced by them. Roosevelt thought that Tolstoy was too detached in dealing with Anna Karenina's adultery, but he was gratified that, in the end, she committed suicide. Whereas Roosevelt had only grudging admiration for *Anna Karenina,* he had unstinted praise for Robert Grant's *Unleavened Bread,* the "strongest study of American life that has been written for many years." Grant's heroine, neglecting the duties of motherhood, descended from the proud security of her home with the inevitability of one of Milton's fallen angels. Judged by similar standards, Edgar Fawcett won Roosevelt's plaudits for his properly vindictive attitude toward the sinful rich. Hamlin Garland, on the other hand, was too "inclined to let certain crude theories warp his mind out of all proper proportion." Clearly Roosevelt believed in the Decalogue and judged in its terms. When the time came, it was natural for him to stand at Armageddon — he had never stood elsewhere.

Roosevelt shared the virulent patriotism of the Civil War generation. His maternal forebears were from the South and the war was in his household. Convinced while a boy of the justice of the Union cause, he welcomed the triumph. After the Union was saved, while the rest of the continent was being conquered, while the products of Mesabi and the open hearth attested to America's growing might, he gloried in the power of his country. National concern over military and physical preparedness, born with the war, soon languished. But Roosevelt, with a few others, kept it alive. His own boyhood fragility, conquered painfully and slowly, and, perhaps, resentment that his father's war service fell to a hired substitute, intensified this legitimate concern. A first venture into history, his study of the War of 1812, supplied further evidence of the national peril in unpreparedness. Darwinian biology substantiated the need for personal physical strength. Taken together, the memories, emotions, and neuroses of childhood, and the historical and biological investigations of youth formed the basis for the cult of strenuosity with which Roosevelt's name is irrevocably linked and for the martial chauvinism which set him apart from most of his moderately nationalistic class. He neither understood nor tolerated the effete in any sphere of activity.

Roosevelt did not consider himself militaristic, but he clearly intended the nation to be both prepared and willing to fight. Enthusiastically embracing the doctrines of Admiral Alfred Thayer Mahan, Roosevelt admonished his countrymen to build up the navy. Elsewhere he urged the individual to improve himself. Through outdoor life and exercise, personal preparedness could be made the handmaiden of national rearmament. With adequate military equipment and a healthy citizenry, the United States could enforce its just demands, could participate as an equal in international affairs.

The combination of white supremacy, national glory, and moral obligation spelled imperialism. Mahan's naval strategy dictated the acquisition of bases in Hawaii, Guam, Cuba, Panama, and Porto Rico. Duty involved the liberation of the Cubans and the enforced improvement of the Filipinos. For these people Roosevelt felt genuine responsibility, insisting that tariff benefits accompany American occupation. While urging the United States to become a colonial power, he also urged the country to cast away the vestiges of colonialism in American diplomacy. Roosevelt respected the British and admired their contributions to

American civilization, but he took an uncompromising position against them when their demands conflicted with his understanding of proper American policies or claims.

Roosevelt's views on foreign affairs, like his moral attitudes, were reflected in his judgment of literature. Literature was to be strenuous and patriotic. He thrilled to any epic of fighting men. In accounts of American feats at arms he took indiscriminate pleasure, for "the man who has in him real fighting blood is sure to be more deeply stirred by the deeds of his own people than by those of any other folk." Conversely, he resented criticism of American manners and American letters. Miss Wilkins made Roosevelt feel "uncomfortable," for he hated "to think that her types are really typical of our life." Frank Norris' "overstatement" was "so preposterous as to deprive his work of all value." The very worst in literature, Roosevelt held, were the products of the expatriates, of whom the worst was Henry James, "thank Heaven . . . now an avowedly British novelist." Roosevelt excoriated James, a "man in whom intense love of country is wanting . . . a very despicable creature, no matter how well equipped with all the minor virtues and graces, literary, artistic, and social." James was a "miserable little snob" whose "polished, pointless, uninteresting stories about the upper social classes of England" made "one blush to think he was once an American." Neither in diplomacy, in international yachting, nor in belles-lettres would Roosevelt tolerate any "strained humility toward foreigners, . . . especially toward Englishmen."

Roosevelt had built an eclectic intellectual home, its parts connected, but the whole more comfortable than integrated. It was designed to provide security for a man whose personality compelled him to act, whose profession required him to compromise, and whose moral beliefs forced him to justify everything he did. There was room for Roosevelt's Darwinism, his social gospel, his chauvinism, and his strenuosity, and these were not tightly compartmented, but related each to the other. Still this complex man was not entirely secure. He had the assurance that comes with great physical courage, but he needed clear and continued evidence of approval. During every campaign he expected defeat. After each victory he was almost pathologically exuberant. His constant motion both released and revealed his constant tension. The violence with which he attacked his critics attested to his doubts. Yet he was sure enough to respond, when challenged, with argument as well as condemnation, and sure enough to act with purpose.

If Roosevelt had any supreme belief it was in character, individual character and national character. Feeling as he did, he was deeply impressed by Brooks Adams' *Law of Civilization and Decay*. He considered the book "brilliant," "very strong." Adams and Roosevelt, with many others of their class, resented the power of the new masters of American industry and finance. These men and their political agents, in the ruthlessness of their struggle for success, had abandoned ethical considerations in business and politics. Their manner of life, private as well as public, offended the sensibilities of more civilized men. To an alarming degree their methods and their taste permeated much of American society on every level. Reacting against this vulgarization, Brooks Adams and his brother Henry foresaw doom; Henry James found etiquette in exile; Roosevelt's friends reminded one another of the gross cunning of international bankers who, as they often pointed out, were, conveniently for the Anglo-American reputation, usually Semitic.

Roosevelt, unlike Henry Adams and Henry James, did not retreat. He met the corrupt as well as the illiterate in political battle. But he shared with the Adamses and James a disdain for the vulgar rich. Their standards, he felt, were the historic ruination of social efficiency. A decade before Brooks Adams published his book, Roosevelt damned the propertied class of revolutionary France, the "despicable beings, the traders and merchants who have forgotten how to fight, the rich who are too timid to guard their wealth, the men of property, large or small, who need peace, and yet have not the sense and courage to be always prepared to conquer it." New York society, both the *nouveaux riches* and "the people of good family" who had been corrupted, Roosevelt declared in 1891, were of this despicable stamp. The fashionable "took little interest in·literature or politics; . . . did not care to explore and hunt and travel in their own country." Instead, "they put wealth above everything else, and therefore hopelessly vulgarized their lives."

Roosevelt, therefore, sympathized strongly with Adams' classifications of the imaginative and the economic man, but he was nonetheless disturbed by Adams' prophetic conclusions. He simply could not admit that the United States was declining nor could he vote for silver at sixteen to one. He declared that Brooks Adams was "a little unhinged." But this was not enough. For his own peace of mind Roosevelt had to demonstrate that Adams' book was "from a false standpoint." Adams had made mistakes. Roosevelt found them. He pointed out that Adams had warped the facts in applying his thesis to Rome. Change from an imaginative to an economic society had occurred during expansion as well as during contraction of the currency. In the decline of Rome the currency factor was less important than the competition of Asiatic and African slaves and cheap Egyptian labor. These doomed the Italian husbandman. In the United States, Roosevelt maintained, emancipation of the slaves, convict labor laws, restriction of Chinese immigration, and the protective tariff prevented competition which might threaten "the free workingman." As for currency, wage earners and farmers in the United States and other "gold" countries stood "waist high above their brothers in Mexico and other communities that use[d] only silver."

Adams' thesis, Roosevelt continued, did not apply at all times or in all places. The Spaniards and Russians of the late nineteenth century, although not economic men, were inferior in martial prowess to the economic men of Germany, England, or the United States. National development need not correlate with economic life. Adams had overlooked more significant factors.

Healthy children, the "virile" qualities, national honor, these were the vital determinants.

Like Brooks Adams, Roosevelt worried about the economic man. Unlike Adams, he was optimistic. He did not expect wealth to continue to corrupt American life because he had faith that men of character would understand the responsibility of power. Where such character was lacking, where the power of wealth was misdirected, Roosevelt was prepared to have the government intercede. Roosevelt was never radical, but, while resisting what seemed to him to be revolution, he welcomed change. From his rudimentary beginnings in the movements for civil service and for slum clearance, enlightened alike by the reformers he fought and the reformers he helped, he developed increasing concern over the abuses of great wealth, increasing inclination to listen, at least, to the demands of organized labor, and increasing determination to invest the state with authority to control the powerful and assist the weak.

During his governorship Roosevelt sustained his beliefs. The times were, it is true, conducive to change, but he played a vital part in developing the spirit of the times. Much of the legislation he sponsored or approved remedied political and social conditions that had attracted his attention years earlier. The achievements of his administration in protecting labor and consumers and in disciplining business, while not spectacular, were substantial. Neither the labor vote, nor machine support, nor campaign contributions sufficiently explain Roosevelt's position. His program, born of conviction as well as expediency, permitted an increase in the sphere of the state's action, subordinating the interests of the individual to those of the community. He had by 1900 effected a synthesis of experience which allowed him to act as well as to believe. He had developed those principles of behavior by which he intended to discipline his use of power. He had begun to apply through politics his standards of national character and social efficiency.

But at all times he knew he needed power — needed it professionally, by temperament needed it almost desperately. He had by 1901 convictions, laboriously formed; he had by then mastered techniques of politics and government; in September of that year he inherited high office. Even then, however, though he was President, he did not have the power he needed. The full use of the techniques, the full application of the convictions, the consummation of his career awaited his demonstration that he could and would rule. Boldly, inexorably, with confident enthusiasm, Roosevelt proceeded at once to stake his precious claim.

Chapter I V

PRESIDENT AND PARTY

The dinner, the story goes, celebrated Roosevelt's appointment in 1906 of Oscar Straus as Secretary of Commerce and Labor. The President explained his choice. He had selected Straus without regard to race, color, creed or party. His concern had been only to find the most qualified man in the United States. This Jacob Schiff would confirm. Schiff, presiding at the celebration, good-naturedly senescent, wealthy, respectable, and, regrettably for Roosevelt, now quite deaf, nodded. "Dot's right, Mr. President," he acknowledged. "You came to me and said, 'Chake, who is der best Jew I can appoint Segretary of Commerce?'" William Loeb, Roosevelt's secretary, persuaded the newspapermen to suppress the exchange.

Doubtless apocryphal, this story nevertheless contains the stuff of authenticity. Aware, as he was, of the political importance of self-conscious groups in American society, Roosevelt throughout his Presidency took care to find important posts for labor leaders, Grand Army men, Hungarian-Americans, Jews, Catholics, and Methodists. Characteristically, in each such case he persuaded himself that he had acted without regard to anything but the best interest of the public. "Now, about my relations with my fellow Americans of Jewish faith," he wrote in 1901. "Really, . . . all that I have done is to treat them precisely and exactly as I treat other Americans." There was enough truth in this meritorious assertion to make it a serviceable fiction. Oscar Straus was by any standard a worthy appointee. If his selection enhanced Republican strength in New York in 1906,

Roosevelt, from his point of view, achieved two worthy ends in one stroke.

A like compatibility, or perhaps confusion, of calculation and conscience eased Roosevelt's quest, begun even before the assassination of McKinley, for nomination and election in 1904. For four years he attended assiduously to this, his happiest campaign. Roosevelt's purpose, like that of any Presidential aspirant, had three parts. He had first to control his party, a process which depended upon his ability to commandeer the agencies of power within it. He had secondly to fashion a program — a record of accomplishment and a charter of intention — at once acceptable to the party and conducive to popular support. He had finally to conduct a winning national canvass. To these ends, with minimal offense to any of them he had to reconcile the conflicting interests of power groups within American society. Were he successful in the first two objectives, the last, when the time came, would be the easiest. But the first two raised large problems.

From McKinley Roosevelt inherited title to both an office and an organization. The office with its great powers was his alone. The organization, for the while, was Hanna's. It could impede Roosevelt's nomination. In Congress it could vitiate his program. Had Roosevelt antagonized it, he would probably have gone the way of his accidental predecessors. While he needed the organization, Roosevelt could not let Hanna's strength go unchallenged. Left to his own devices Hanna might have turned the party in 1904 toward a new McKinley or even toward himself. Roosevelt, who wished always to rule as well as to reign, could tolerate no division of power between the White House and the senator's suite at the Arlington Hotel. "Uncle Mark," who may have cared little about reigning, had become accustomed to rule. Senator Matthew Quay described the situation precisely. There was going to be trouble, he predicted, because "we have two Executive Mansions."

Theodore Roosevelt and Marcus Alonzo Hanna, superficially so different, were in many ways very like, particularly in their thinking on public policy. Hearst's familiar caricature of "Dollar Mark" — a bloated capitalist whose distended paunch stretched a garish vest resplendent with dollar signs, whose foot trod heavily upon the attenuated anatomy of some poor farmer or workingman, whose gross mouth curved contemptuously around a pure Havana corona — confirmed only the prejudices of Populism. The contributors to Republican campaign funds, never contemptuous in company with a Havana corona, knew Hanna better than did Hearst. Indisputably, irrevocably, he cherished the gold standard. But, they knew, he had in 1894 damned George Pullman even as national troops quieted Pullman's strikers. Like Roosevelt, Hanna stoutly denied that an omniscient "God in His infinite wisdom" had "given the control of the property interests" to the bulls and the Baers. From the Civic Federation of which Hanna was the active president Roosevelt freely borrowed ideas on the control of corporations and the relations of labor and capital which would have alarmed the ogre Hearst painted. Hanna of his own will supported Roosevelt's policies on the Cuban tariff, conservation, and the liquidation of the Northern Securities Company, the first trust Roosevelt busted. "No man," Roosevelt recalled, "had larger traits than Hanna. He was a big man in every way and as forceful a personality as we have seen in public life in our generation. I think that not merely I myself, but the whole party and the whole country have reason to be very grateful to him for the way in which, after I came into office, under circumstances which were very hard for him, he resolutely declined to be drawn into the position which a smaller man of meaner cast would inevitably have taken; that is, the position of antagonizing public policies if I was identified with them."

The fat old senator in the wrinkled gray suit and the stout young President in the muddied riding breeches differed, essentially, not over policies but over power. Both wanted to control the Republican party. Hanna in September 1901 had control. Roosevelt had the power to gain control. They had no way, in their parts, to compromise their difference; they had no particular need to discuss it. They could manage, therefore, a guarded friendship, a genuine mutual respect, a continual, cautious alliance for common causes. But below the surface of this uneasy relationship, often elusively, observing at all times the niceties of political diplomacy, avoiding at all costs a declared war, the publicity it would have entailed, and the debilitation it would have caused the instrument for which he contended, Roosevelt for two years engaged in an accelerated race for arms. Equally diplomatic, equally elusive, equally concerned with protecting the party, Hanna, confronted by an aggressor who had every advantage, quietly tightened his lines until, ultimately, to protect his home district he surrendered his ambition for any larger domain.

The heart of Hanna's organization beat in the Middle West. There a combination of little-known state leaders in 1896 and 1900 had mustered votes which wrested the national conventions from the hands of more celebrated bosses of the East. Among others, Senator Wolcott of Colorado, Richard C. Kerens of Missouri, Cyrus Leland of Kansas rendered services to Hanna and McKinley for which they were well rewarded. Touching off a direct assault against Hanna's reliable center, Roosevelt boldly invaded the domains of these men.

With almost indecent haste, Roosevelt commenced mobilization a few days after taking his oath of office. "I greatly wish to consult you about the Colorado appointments," he wrote Philip B. Stewart in September 1901. Stewart, whose "sweetness and high-minded disinterestedness" did not, it developed, impair his politicking, was one of those men with whom Roosevelt, while still Vice-President, had begun to plan for 1904. Those plans could now be furthered, especially in the unstable political environment of Colorado. There during the '90s both major parties had divided on the silver issue, the Silver Republicans and Silver Democrats combining with the Populists against a fluctuating coalition of sound-money forces. By 1901, with silver a dead issue, these coalitions were disintegrating as traditional party lines were reëstablished. In the Republican party, the rivalries of ambitious local leaders combined with past differences over silver to produce disequilibrium. Hanna had nurtured the Republican faction led by Senator Wolcott and the state chairman. Their use of his support, however, had embittered a considerable opposition including both disgruntled politicians and various personal friends of Roosevelt like Stewart. Making only a gesture of consulting Wolcott, Roosevelt turned more and more to the senator's opponents. Before July 1903, new officials, selected by the President on the advice of these men, had replaced Wolcott's allies as custodians of the mint and customhouse at Denver. In these important federal posts the politician in command had under his direction scores of employees who could work political wonders in their precincts. Thus armed, Stewart and his associates guaranteed Colorado's support for Roosevelt's nomination.

To overturn Hanna in Kansas the President overrode the counsel of his loyal friend, William Allen White, the Emporia editor and local savant, who had early taken an oath of allegiance to Roosevelt for 1904. White was inordinately fond of Cyrus Leland, the professional Grand Army Republican and conservative state boss who had worked with Hanna. Leland, White urged, provided an indispensable bulwark against Kansas Senator Joseph R. Burton, a former Populist turned Republican, later (as White predicted) a convicted thief. Yet Roosevelt, concluding that Leland and Burton were "two of a kind, or almost of a kind," in his first two years in office usually honored Burton's wishes on patronage. He would not, he explained to White, fight with a senator except on a matter of principle. His controlling but unexplained principle, moreover, was apparently the destruction of Leland, for every important federal official in Kansas whose appointment was considered a senatorial prerogative was displaced. One of these was Leland himself. His post as Commissioner of Pensions for the Missouri Valley Roosevelt conferred upon a veteran of the Spanish War, long a regular Republican, whom Burton and the Kansas national committeeman had endorsed. When this appointment was announced, White recalled, "the members of the G.A.R. in Emporia came out . . . like a swarm of bees, buzzing their anger." They buzzed in vain. With Leland stripped of power, Roosevelt felt secure in Kansas. White and the G.A.R. he would compensate in time.

So it was in Missouri also. There for over a decade the direction of federal patronage had belonged to Republican National Committeeman Richard C. Kerens, an Irish-Catholic immigrant who had amassed a fortune in railroading and lumbering. An able executive, a generous contributor to party funds, and a valued collaborator of Hanna, Kerens enjoyed the authority to which, he felt, he had become continuously entitled. Roosevelt, however, chose to innovate. For the most part ignoring Kerens, he dispensed patronage according to the advice of the Missouri Republican congressmen, of the publisher of the influential, independent Kansas City *Evening Star,* and of a conspicuous and demanding member of the Roosevelt-for-President Club. Over half of the key federal offices in Missouri changed hands. Roosevelt's supporters, sustained by federal aid and astutely led by the President's appointee as Assistant Treasurer of the United States at St. Louis, gained control of the state committee in 1902. At once they forced Kerens and his associates to agree to a formal endorsement of Roosevelt for the nomination in 1904.

In Colorado, Kansas, and Missouri Roosevelt attended to the details of manipulation that elsewhere he ordinarily assigned to the members of his political staff. They, like the President, worked by preference with proved Republicans but with Republicans unconnected with Hanna and the McKinley regime. Each member of the President's council had special knowledge or special experience for his specific functions in reconstructing the party. Highest ranking was Henry Clay Payne of Wisconsin, appointed Postmaster General in December 1901 to replace a pro-Hanna New Yorker whose local political influence Roosevelt did not need. An Old Guard Republican, Payne had many enemies within and without the party. Robert La Follette and his progressive associates in Wisconsin, already disturbed by Roosevelt's reliance upon the powerful, conservative senator from their state, were chagrined by the promotion of Payne, another traditional enemy. Labor, still angry about Payne's intransigence during a Milwaukee streetcar strike in 1896, was offended. Yet Roosevelt considered the new Postmaster General an asset. Whatever the merits of the Wisconsin progressives, the President needed the coöperation and confidence of conservative Republicans whose strength for the time precluded battle. Payne commanded that confidence. Furthermore, he was willing to challenge Hanna. Even before 1900 he had sponsored Roosevelt for President. Widely experienced in politics, he could be trusted with the delicate task of advising all the executive departments on the distribution of patronage. He understood not only the Middle West but also the East and, most important, the South, where on the precinct level Hanna's agents had to be either won over or supplanted. Because of his office and talents the key political figure in the Cabinet, Payne could muster an energetic corps for Roosevelt in 1904.

With a lesser portfolio than Payne's, James S. Clarkson brought his furtive energies to the President's quest. Rescuing that tested spoilsman of the Harrison administration from the oblivion where Hanna had carefully confined him, Roosevelt made Clarkson Surveyor of the Port of New York. To the alarmed proponents of civil service who condemned this appointment, Roosevelt replied that Clarkson's announced intention of adhering to civil service principles revealed "a rather good spirit." That spirit, however, never inhibited Clarkson on his unofficial errands in three vital areas. In the Middle West, especially in his native Iowa, Clarkson exercised political influence through the National Republican League which, in many places, was supplanting the state organizations as the party agency. At his direction the league acted to cement alliances between businessmen and the Republican party. This was a useful makeweight for Roosevelt who worried constantly about the apparently growing enthusiasm of the financial community for Hanna. In New York, with Roosevelt's appointee as Collector of the Port, Clarkson steadied the President's personal forces. Finally, as he had for Harrison, Clarkson stood a practiced guard over the wavering Republicans of the South. His familiarity with that area equipped him to discover and resist any incipient Hanna movement. A veteran of post-bellum Dixie politics, long a friend of Negro Republicans, Clarkson took particular pleasure in converting organizations which Hanna had made "lily white" to the "black and tan" of the carpetbag tradition. From such changes Roosevelt gained idealistic as well as political satisfaction.

The South no less than the Middle West had supplied Hanna with the votes to control national conventions. Federal officeholders in the South, moreover, selected too often only because of their ability to deliver votes, were as a group notoriously third rate. Roosevelt therefore set out to improve the federal service there even as he captured the Republican party. To assist Payne and Clarkson in this mission the President recruited the preëminent Negro leader of his generation, Booker T. Washington. At Roosevelt's invitation Washington dined at the White House on October 16, 1901. The clamor of Southern whites over the racial implications of this dinner obscured the immediate significance of the occasion. Washington's mission was political. Roosevelt found him always a useful counselor on Southern appointments. Distrustful of Southern Populists who had exploited racial prejudices, Washington encouraged Roosevelt to appoint both conservative Democrats and Negro Republicans of more versatile talents than most of those recommended by Clarkson. But state by state, while he tried to give the Negro a fairer share of offices, while he endeavored to improve the federal service, Roosevelt managed invariably either to win over Hanna's liegemen or to replace them.

In South Carolina the President found John G. Capers, a Confederate veteran and Gold Democrat who had left his party to support McKinley, "already installed as the nominal head of the republican organization." "I took him as my adviser," Roosevelt observed, "and ruthlessly threw out all the old republican politicians." To a few vacancies thus created Roosevelt appointed Negroes, including one whose nomination for Collector of the Port of Charleston touched off an interminable struggle in the Senate. This nomination Roosevelt interpreted as an issue in race equality, but he also instructed his nominee to "keep in close touch" with Capers. To most of the vacancies Roosevelt named white men, "three-fourths of them were democrats, for the most part sons or daughters of ex-Confederates, or themselves ex-Confederates." This was perhaps a milestone on the Road to Reunion. It was more than that: Hanna's agent in South Carolina, the chairman of the Republican State Committee, lobbied unsuccessfully against the new appointments. The President's recruits, he knew, provided the stuff of a loyal personal machine for Capers and Roosevelt.

A new order came also to Louisiana. There Roosevelt replaced Hanna's patronage arbiter with a man of his own choosing, and on his advice and Washington's in 1902 made wholesale changes affecting two thirds of the major federal officials under the justice and treasury departments. In two cases evidence of misconduct in office provided cause for change. Otherwise Roosevelt simply got rid of the incumbents as their terms in office expired. The director of the reconstructed Republican organization in Louisiana grieved the President by excluding Negroes from his councils, but he delivered an enthusiastic Roosevelt delegation to the convention of 1904.

In Alabama where Hanna had used white Republicans to manage the party Roosevelt turned toward the colored. Advised by Washington, Clarkson, and Payne, Roosevelt appointed only those whites who were willing, superficially at least, to share control of the party with Negroes. One of these appointees, United States Judge Thomas G. Jones, from his bench struck compelling blows against Negro peonage. The United States

Attorney in Jones' district, a selection of Clarkson, made his mark in politics. From Roosevelt's point of view, the South needed both men.

Many of Hanna's agents, some of them men of power, retained their jobs. This was particularly true in Georgia. The leading Negro Republican there, an open advocate of Hanna for President, in December 1901 expected to lose his position as Register of the Treasury. He asked Booker T. Washington to persuade Roosevelt to keep him in office. Perhaps impressed by the man's frankness about Hanna, Roosevelt granted his request. He also reappointed two other pro-Hanna Georgia Negroes. After their reappointments, these men, possibly grateful, possibly thinking of the future, became less contentious than they had earlier been. Neutralization by reward, Roosevelt realized, was a kinder device, but as effective a one, as condign punishment by expulsion.

Roosevelt prided himself on his Southern appointments. "It is in my mind equally an outrage against the principles of our party and of our government," he maintained, "to appoint an improper man to a position because he is a Negro, or with a view of affecting the Negro vote; or on the other hand, to exclude a proper man from an office or as a delegate because he is a Negro. I shall never knowingly consent to either doctrine." Essentially he observed this tenet; he discriminated not on the basis of color but on the basis of Hanna. From that discrimination, however, the Negro gained less than the President persuaded himself he had offered. Roosevelt referred constantly to his wisdom in giving office to respectable Gold Democrats and to men of good family. Their appointments, incontrovertibly happy developments for federal administration in the South, were nevertheless not as altruistic as Roosevelt sometimes suggested. He hoped, by his own account, that in the border states defections of Gold Democrats to the Republicans might turn the balance of power. In any Southern state, he preferred "imaginative" Gold Democrats to "economic" Hanna Republicans. Yet strange man that he was, Roosevelt could not admit to himself

— and he certainly never suggested — that the one consistent, continuing result of his Southern patronage policies was his surer control of the Republican party.

The most important of the Eastern Republican organizations Hanna had never controlled. It was, in fact, a triumph of his political genius that he engineered McKinley's nomination in 1896 without the help of Pennsylvania and New York, states whose large populations gave them outstanding weight within the national convention as well as in the electoral college. In Pennsylvania the dominant personality in Republican politics for two decades had been Senator Matthew S. Quay, a manager of Harrison's campaigns, never reconciled to Hanna's rule. To demonstrate his independence of Hanna, Quay in 1900 had helped arrange Roosevelt's nomination for Vice-President. Thereafter Roosevelt more or less counted upon the support of Quay and his colleague for 1904. He assured their allegiance by deferring to their requests on patronage. An ally of Quay succeeded a well-regarded proponent of civil service reform as Collector of Internal Revenue in Philadelphia. Another of Quay's associates became postmaster in that city. While bluestocking Philadelphia goo-goos still gasped, in 1902 Quay easily persuaded the Pennsylvania Republican State Convention to endorse Roosevelt for nomination in 1904.

New York Roosevelt handled gingerly. Although Hanna had no useful agent there, the state was by no means secure, and New York's support, valuable to any Presidential aspirant, was indispensable to a native son. Within the Republican party in New York Senator Platt's authority had been threatened by his former ally, elected governor in 1900, Benjamin B. Odell. While Platt's gradual decline tended to free Roosevelt of an ancient incubus, Odell's gradual ascendancy created a new and ruthless rival who cherished Presidential ambitions of his own. As ever, Platt was a "mite apprehensive" about Roosevelt, and Odell at times was openly hostile. Neither could be relied upon. Yet, to keep New York from the Democrats Roosevelt had to persuade, sometimes to force the two to coöperate. While so doing, while preserving as well as he could a balance of power between Platt and Odell, the President built a third force. His intricate, incessant maneuverings to these ends, too involved to merit detailed recounting, depended upon his distribution of federal patronage in relatively equal parts to the senator, to the governor, and to his own lieutenants.

In building for himself Roosevelt avoided association with New York City's reform mayor and his independent supporters. He had, of course, unofficial advisers — like Nicholas Murray Butler, the president of Columbia University — who were independent Republicans, but he either recruited or trained professional Republicans to serve his interests in the state. Of these professionals, the first chosen were James S. Clarkson, Collector of the Port of New York, Nevada N. Stranahan, who had demonstrated his loyalty and political talent during Roosevelt's governorship, and Joseph Murray, since 1881 the original Roosevelt man, now appointed Deputy Commissioner of Immigration at Ellis Island. These men and their subordinates in 1902 helped to secure the nomination for lieutenant governor of a tested friend of the President, and, in spite of the opposition of Platt, to put through the state convention a resolution which, albeit equivocally, endorsed Roosevelt for 1904.

Roosevelt had also chosen two younger men on whom he planned to confer direction of his affairs in New York: Assemblyman James W. Wadsworth, Jr., an upstate Republican, later a congressman and United States Senator; and Herbert Parsons, a wealthy Manhattan lawyer and alderman, later a congressman and the chairman of the New York County Republican Committee. Parsons' serious indoctrination began in 1903. "This is to introduce to you Mr. Herbert Parsons," Roosevelt then wrote Clarkson. "He is one of the men in whom I have taken a real interest, because I feel that you must depend upon him and his kind to get the republican organization in New York City on a footing of real usefulness and power. He is also one of the men whom I should suggest for the carrying out of your idea as regards getting an active organization of zealous, genuine republicans to work in New York City during the Presidential campaign next year. I cordially commend him to you and hope you can help him and will consult with him." Clarkson complied. In time Parsons succeeded his instructor as the President's agent in the city. For the while pupil and teacher worked together successfully to ensure New York for Roosevelt well before the Republicans met in Chicago to decide the nomination of 1904.

Clearly, throughout the United States, Roosevelt from the time he became President constructed a personal organization within the Republican party. In most states the simple fact that he was President and had the political power of that office sufficed to convince the existing local organizations of his availability for nomination. In those states where prior allegiances to a local leader either ambitious himself or beholden to Hanna impeded his purpose, Roosevelt proselyted effectively. To do so he did not need to invade the classified service — most of the politically influential federal offices were still unclassified. And as Roosevelt pointed out, "public servants . . . without the classified service . . . are as a rule chosen largely with reference to political considerations, and as a rule are and expect to be changed with the change of parties." As the party of Roosevelt succeeded the party of Hanna and McKinley, the President, respecting the traditional prerogatives of the Senate, consulted the Republican senators about his appointments and, where possible, followed their wishes. He consulted also their established organizations, but, he wrote: "It is one thing to say that I shall consult the organization in making appointments; it is an entirely different thing to say that I shall consult no one but the organization . . ." Hanna and his allies spoke frequently, but only occasionally did they have the last word.

Roosevelt in his appointments probably raised the level of competency not only on the federal bench, where his selections were almost without exception excellent, but also in those offices normally political sinecures. "Character and capacity" can, after all, accompany loyal partisanship. He could and did joke about his manipulations. "I think I shall now try to find out who were the political heelers responsible for your appointment," Roosevelt wrote Oliver Wendell Holmes, Jr., the great jurist whom he had appointed to the Supreme Court, "that I may ask them to see that you swing your wards properly this fall."

But where Clarkson and his likes were concerned, the swinging of wards was no joke. The Gold Democrats, the mentors of Harrison now returned to power, the political friends — hard-shell veterans and reform-minded rookies alike — whom Roosevelt appointed to key positions understood without explicit Presidential directions that they were to press Roosevelt's nomination and election. Their success in controlling the state conventions that endorsed the President as early as 1902 and in assisting the victorious Republican congressional campaigners in that year attested to their efficiency. Enthroned by accident, Roosevelt none the less obviously intended to be king.

Mark Hanna's intentions were as cloudy as Roosevelt's were clear. Still chairman of the Republican National Committee, still a power in the Senate, again and again mentioned as the pre-ferred candidate of Wall Street for the Presidency, Hanna might have thrown down the gage of battle a dozen different times. Yet not only did he support Roosevelt's policies but he also fought none of his political appointments. He did lead the op-position to Roosevelt's nomination of Leonard Wood — the first colonel of the President's beloved Rough Riders — for a major generalship, but this episode, so fraught with bad feeling, had small meaning, if any, for the suzerainty of the Republican party. In the Wood case Hanna may have acted as he did simply to oppose the President's personal friend; more likely, demonstrat-ing the loyalty downward of a good politician, he objected to Wood's promotion because one of his retainers had clashed with the general in Cuba. Before and after the Wood affair Hanna, posturing a simple, solid dignity, without comment watched his authority within the party dwindle. He had no weapons with which to strike back effectively, no patronage to dispense, no prestige comparable to Roosevelt's. He might, of course, have led a revolt anyhow, but against such a resourceful politician as Roosevelt this would have been futile. Mark Hanna never attempted the futile.

While Hanna would not counterattack, neither would he capitulate. Although he repeatedly stated his indifference to the Presidential nomination, he refused to commit himself to Roosevelt's candidacy. No one will ever know whether Hanna wanted to be President. Always, however, more than any office he preferred to have the determining part in the direction of the Republican party. This in itself was enough to make him distrust Roosevelt. It was also enough to impel Roosevelt, who personified all issues, to make Hanna the objective correlative of the elements in the party he feared. The senator's ambivalence about the nomination evidenced his continuing independence. As long as he refused to endorse Roosevelt, so long was Roosevelt's nomination susceptible to organized opposition. Over the endorsement, therefore, their rivalry came to focus. On that issue at last they clashed.

The occasion for their collision was cleverly contrived by Joseph Benson Foraker, senior senator from Ohio, long Hanna's aggressive rival there. At the Ohio Republican Convention in May 1903 Foraker submitted a resolution praising Roosevelt's administration and endorsing him for President in 1904. If the resolution passed, it blocked opposition by Ohio to Roosevelt. It gave Foraker prestige as the Roosevelt protagonist in the state. It bound Hanna at least to neutrality, thereby removing him both as a candidate and as a leader of resistance. Two of Hanna's aides had recently proposed him for the Presidency. Even if he had not authorized their action, he was not ready to deny himself freedom of action in 1904. Yet Hanna was reluctant to fight the resolution directly or without the President's consent. He did not wish to break with Roosevelt whom he might eventually want to support. Nor could he in 1903 afford a break, for he needed the assistance of the administration in his forthcoming race for the Senate against a popular liberal Democrat. Finally, his primacy within the party in Ohio would be jeopardized if Roosevelt were to strengthen the Foraker faction.

In this uncomfortable pass, Hanna wired the President: "The issue which has been forced on me in the matter of our State Convention this year endorsing you for the Republican nomination next year has come in a way which makes it necessary for me to oppose such a resolution. When you know all the facts I am sure you will approve my course." The local ramifications of Foraker's maneuver, Hanna suggested to the press, forced his stand. Furthermore, he explained, as a matter of principle he considered the endorsement premature. This last was hardly convincing. Over twenty states had already endorsed Roosevelt. And in 1887 and 1895 Ohio Republicans, at the direction of Hanna, had committed themselves a year in advance of national conventions.

Roosevelt did not permit Hanna to escape from the trap Foraker had set. "The time had come," he decided, "to stop shilly-shallying, and let Hanna know definitely that I did not intend to assume the position, at least passively, of a suppliant to whom he might give the nomination as a boon." Hanna had told the press that he would oppose the resolution, but he had not made public his telegram to the President. Roosevelt at once released his reply to that still confidential telegram: "I have not asked any man for his support. I have had nothing whatever to do with raising this issue. Inasmuch as it has been raised of course those who favor my administration and my nomination will favor endorsing both and those who do not will oppose." Since open warfare was for Hanna both premature and intolerable, he could now only surrender. "I shall not," he wired the President, "oppose the endorsement of your administration and candidacy by our State Convention."

The political cognoscenti enjoyed a "good chuckle over Hanna's 'back-action-double-spring feat.'" For the senator, however, it could have been no laughing matter. The exchange of telegrams was public acknowledgement that an exchange of power had taken place in the Republican party. After the episode there was no discernible alteration in the relations of the two principals, but there was clearly only one executive mansion. Roosevelt was frankly "pleased at the outcome." "It simplified things all around," he wrote Henry Cabot Lodge, "for in my judgment Hanna was my only formidable opponent so far as the nomination . . . [was] concerned."

The chase had still a way to run, for if Hanna no longer could outwardly oppose, neither would he openly support Roosevelt's nomination. Assisted by the President, Hanna won his campaign for reëlection. When victory revived talk of the senator's availability for higher office, Roosevelt advised Hanna to declare that he was not a candidate. Hanna refused. "In strict confidence" Roosevelt interpreted this exchange. Hanna, he concluded, was "letting 'I dare not' wait upon 'I would' . . . and while he still half hopes to make a candidate he will not take any such action as I have advised." The President therefore pursued his earlier advantage. One tactic he had initiated at the time of the Ohio convention: "I have had a great reception here in the West," he then confided to Lodge, "and yesterday at Spokane made what I consider my best speech . . . I made it particularly with reference to having a knockdown and dragout fight with Hanna and the whole Wall Street crowd . . ." Increasingly Roosevelt publicly identified Hanna with the New York bankers — those persistent bogeymen of American campaigns. He also struck Hanna once more in Ohio. Early in January 1904 three Ohio postmasters of Hanna's choosing were replaced by adherents of Foraker.*

* The turnover in Ohio was sheer manipulation, but in 1903 and 1904 Roosevelt for disinterested reasons incidentally rid the postal service of several of Hanna's friends. The hard core of morality in Roosevelt, his deep interest in decency in government, his realization that only an honest staff could be entrusted with the functions he wished government to assume,

By the end of January Roosevelt was confident. "I can tell you," he wrote a friend, "that outside all the Southern States I am now as certain as I well can be that if Hanna made the fight, and with all the money of Wall Street behind him, he would get the majority of the delegation from no State excepting Ohio; and from the South I should have from a third to a half of the delegates, and most of the remainder would have been pledged to me . . . I believe that the best advisers among my opponents themselves see this and have very nearly made up their minds to give up the contest."

This prophecy was never tested, for Hanna died. With his death, what remained of Roosevelt's opposition, deprived of leadership, collapsed. Perhaps Hanna himself had never seriously encouraged that opposition. He had been shorn of his power, however, because until the end he alone was equipped to contest the nomination of the determined incumbent, and until then he would not renounce that potential. Hanna's death clinched Roosevelt's control of the party. Still Roosevelt found it "very sad," for the enigmatic senator, however unwilling to surrender authority, had been a considerable figure among the Republicans who facilitated those accomplishments on which, vigorously, Roosevelt would go to the cheering people. Their enthusiasm the President had been cultivating carefully.

---

made him a relentless persecutor of the men in the Post Office Department, many of them high-ranking officials, whose fraudulent activities were exposed in 1903. The removal of those who happened to be friends of Hanna had value for the President within the party. His larger political gain, however, was probably simply the popularity that attends the discovery and punishment of corruption in high places. Even before the invention of television, such action furnished salutary matter for national campaigns, particularly for those, like Roosevelt, who advertised well.

Chapter V

PRESIDENT AND PEOPLE

"*There is also another side to be remembered,*" Roosevelt wrote William Allen White while they corresponded about ways in which to win the leaders of the party for the nomination of 1904. "If my nomination is to come at all, it has to come at the initiative of the people. I know that this has rather a demagogic sound, but I do not mean it in a demagogic way. What I mean is that I want it understood that the prime movers in forcing my nomination are men like you . . . , like the farmers, small businessmen and upper-class mechanics who are my natural allies — I mean who are naturally against populism and who sympathize with my appeal for common sense, courage and common honesty. I expect, or at least I hope, to have on my side the man of intellect who does not sit in his own parlor but who actually goes out and tries to accomplish things. I also hope to have the man of less intellect but who is fundamentally sound, morally, mentally and physically. I want to make it evident that I am pushed by the professional politicians in response to the pressure from these kinds of men and not merely on their own initiative."

Roosevelt, the heroic image of the constituency he wished, the active "man of intellect," "sound, morally, mentally and physically," captured the loyalty of the people as had no incumbent President since Andrew Jackson. His policies and the devices of leadership by which he made them the law of the land had of themselves constructive purpose. Yet the man and his policies, taken together, had also an appeal which was, as he meant it to be, a vital ingredient in his political effort. Roosevelt was never a mere sounding board for the popular mind. He had, rather, in his halcyon days, an absolute sense of political pitch. He struck the notes that the chorus awaited. This he did intuitively, for he contained within him the best and the worst of America, the whole spectrum from practical enlightenment and sound moral judgment to sentimentalism and braggadocio. He could touch greatness and he could skirt cheapness. Lincoln Steffens, with characteristically half-true discernment, postulated that Roosevelt thought with his hips. This was true insofar as Roosevelt anticipated unerringly, often subconsciously, the wishes of the bulk of Americans. Consciously he did not "mean it in a demagogic way." But the result was wonderful at the polls.

"Common sense, courage and common honesty," buttressed with the fervent pleas for motherhood that Roosevelt issued with righteous repetition, colored his platform with the splendor of Bryan's revivalist imagery. It was, after all, part of the national faith to believe in the "Square Deal" even before Roosevelt so named it. Roosevelt had, moreover, before he stumped the land, herded cattle, captured outlaws, been a kind of policeman, and — single-handed — killed a Spaniard. Not even an urban childhood, myopia, a Harvard degree, a few published books, and tea with Henry Adams damaged those incomparable qualifications. Between the war with Spain and the war in Europe the average American boy, discarding the log cabin and the split rail, adopted a new model of successful conduct — a model that his father, however he voted, cheered throatily and his mother, however she worshiped, endorsed. Even the most partisan, most loyal supporter of Woodrow Wilson confessed unashamed when Roosevelt died that America had loved him.

The "farmers, small businessmen and upper-class mechanics," Roosevelt's "natural allies," in 1904 cheered his deeds as well as the man. Mr. Dooley, that inimitable commentator on American politics, ascertained a certain ambivalence in Roosevelt's attitude toward the trusts, those "heejous monthsters." Mr. Dooley was correct, but his unreflective friend Hinnissy was no less impressed for that. The President had demonstrated, for the first time since it passed in 1890, the power of the Sherman Antitrust Act. He did so by attacking the Northern Securities Company, a combination of railroads each element of which had, in varying degree, incurred the hostility of the farmers in the areas through which it ran. The Northern Securities Company itself was a holding company which, small businessmen knew from a shocked press, had been formed only after a clash of financial giants on the stock market had precipitated the short-lived but fearful panic of 1901. Oliver Wendell Holmes, Jr., dissenting from the decision which ordered the company dissolved, judged that the popular passions surrounding the Northern Securities Case impelled the Supreme Court to distort the law. Those very passions, perhaps, had persuaded Hanna, even before Roosevelt moved, that the negotiators of the merger might have to be disciplined. There were, as they elaborated, large economic benefits in the new company. There were also, as Roosevelt later told Congress, compelling reasons for railroad combinations. But Hinnissy and his kind, the farmers, the mechanics, the small businessmen, usually uninformed about the advantages of an integrated transportation empire and the problems of joint costs in rate-making, saw in the President's celebrated action only a blow for the oppressed against their oppressors who seemed to juggle the stock market and to charge too much to carry grain to seaboard.

Hinnissy's fraternity also applauded the antitrust legislation passed at Roosevelt's behest in 1903. If Mr. Dooley raised a skeptical eyebrow at the President's program which the Attorney General, a conservative corporation lawyer, had drafted, the New York *Sun* spoke vociferously for the element of the business community that damned the program as reckless reform. It had three parts: the Elkins Act forbade rebates; the Expedition Act gave priority to the adjudication of antitrust cases; the act establishing the Department of Commerce and Labor also created the Bureau of Corporations, an agency empowered to investigate and report on the activities of corporations. This whole program, conforming to the most modest recommendations of the Chicago

Conference on Trusts of 1899, was so close to the center of American opinion that the majority of Republicans, including congressmen for whom change was painful, could support or at least condone it. It left unseemly gaps in the federal government's control over industry and transportation. Yet because it provided an entering wedge for that control, it provoked a reactionary resistance on which Roosevelt cleverly capitalized. During the debate on the Bureau of Corporations, he released documents demonstrating that the Rockefellers objected to it. This speeded Roosevelt's program to completion. It did more, for it seemed to prove his continual assertion that he sought only to prevent the excesses of irresponsible wealth. The honest corporation, he had promised, had nothing to fear, but the demoniac trust of the Nast cartoons, the "malefactors of great wealth" he would crush underfoot.

The President's impressively large public could imagine its own malefactors. It did not know that Roosevelt *in camera* had assured J. Pierpont Morgan that the United States Steel Corporation, the largest holding company in America, was safe. Even if it had known, it might not have cared, for it remembered that the President had attacked the Northern Securities Company and the beef trust — two of the largest of the malefactors, both involved immediately in their operations with recognizable living expenses — and that he had grafted on the statute books the weapons for further attacks. Because Roosevelt made those impressions so vivid, few were as skeptical as Mr. Dooley. Most could and did conclude that at last a Saint George had arisen to strike the dragon of privilege from the temple of democracy. The spirit so whetted gave incalculable impetus to the reform movements of the early century. It also provided an irrepressible force, channeled easily by veteran politicians, for the mandate of 1904.

To that mandate the "upper-class mechanics," the trade unions and their leaders, contributed. When Roosevelt took office the sharpest memory of Presidential intervention in a labor conflict was that of Grover Cleveland's peremptory military and legal aid to management during the Pullman strike of 1894. Roosevelt had then praised Cleveland, but in 1902, when he interceded during the strike of anthracite coal miners, he placed his strength behind an arbitration which management resisted. This was not a radical action. The United Mine Workers had grievances so just that arbitration seemed unreasonable only to men like George F. Baer, the reactionary president of the Reading Railroad who worshiped the rich idol of *laissez faire*. Baer and his fellows, unequivocally self-righteous, stubbornly postponed settlement so long that the nation, facing a shortage of coal, became unusually sympathetic to the strikers and gratefully enthusiastic over Roosevelt's ultimately successful efforts to terminate the dispute by referring the issues to an arbitral commission. Baer's obduracy, the reasonableness of the miners, and the national temper persuaded many of the Old Guard and even J. P. Morgan and his partners to support the President. Hanna rendered such invaluable assistance that at the end of the strike Roosevelt observed that "Uncle Mark's work has borne fruit." Yet Roosevelt, far more than his collaborators, received the credit he deserved for making his office an instrument of justice rather than oppression.

Roosevelt never truckled to the labor vote. Toward the syndicalist miners' union of Colorado he exhibited a repressive antagonism born of fear and repugnance. Sharing his attitude toward violence and radicalism in the labor movement, the chiefs of the American Federation of Labor did not protest against his use of troops or his hyperbolic expressions. They did, however, oppose Roosevelt's reinstatement of a nonunion worker in the Government Printing Office. Roosevelt then insisted upon an open shop for all government employees. This not only seriously offended the A.F. of L., but also provoked spirited resistance from Mark Hanna, who was moved as much by principle as by political advantage. Roosevelt endangered his reputation among laboring men by discharging from federal employment the former Grand

Master of the Knights of Labor. He more than compensated, perhaps, by appointing to lucrative positions two officials of the important railroad brotherhoods. Yet these episodes, however much they helped or hurt him, probably carried less weight than his intercession in the anthracite strike. Roosevelt then, of course, understood the importance of the labor vote, but indisputably he acted to realize commendable convictions. Inevitably he performed dramatically. Obviously he did not mean it in a demagogic way.

This was the particular genius of Theodore Roosevelt: to achieve dramatically those ends he valued and thereby, often without any but an intuitive, unconscious purpose, to increase his political capital. Roosevelt had defined for himself an imprecise line between the "lunatic fringe" he detested and the "selfish rich" he despised. Equally to each of these extremes he was anathema. To many wholly sane but more impatient reformers he seemed insincere. To the inert he seemed mad. Most of early-century America, however, agreed with or at least voted for his Square Deal. This was of course his intention, yet he also intended that the salvation of America was to be justice to all classes. Roosevelt made no secret of this even when he was trying to identify Hanna with the "whole Wall Street crowd." Explaining the purpose of one speech he made at that time, the President wrote: "I wished the labor people absolutely to understand that I set my face like flint against violence and lawlessness of any kind on their part, just as much as against arrogant greed by the rich . . ."

Odysseus-like, Roosevelt had long steered between the Scylla and Charybdis he here again identified. The convictions of his youth had charted his continuous course. His jagged dread of violent revolution, his aristocrat's disdain for the hauteur of wealth newly won, fixed at any time his safe position. But surest of all, by politics he found his way. He preached, partly by instinct, partly by design, what the self-conscious middle class, a safe majority, believed. Thereby he attended not only his own career but also the classic mission of politics, the peaceful reconciliation of conflicting interests.

Since the farmers, the mechanics, and the small businessmen, during the four decades before Roosevelt became President, had received too often something less than justice, he had, in order to balance the national scales, frequently to be their champion. At no time did he propose to push the scales past the point of equilibrium, but simply to reach equilibrium he adopted in his first term those positive policies toward labor and corporations with which the Square Deal is associated. Consequently he expected "the criminal rich and the fool rich" to "do all they can to beat me." Doubtless he overestimated their response. Without tipping the scales in the other direction, without sponsoring either radical unionism or the closed shop, without indiscriminately busting every trust, he expected those he helped to rally to his side. Many of them did. The head of the United Mine Workers, for one, cast an ardent Republican vote in 1904 and again in 1908.

The Square Deal incidentally disarmed the Democrats. The new Saint George, as William Jennings Bryan complained, had stolen the lance with which the Great Commoner had twice campaigned. Bryan's party, weary of defeat under his reforming, earthy aegis, fell in 1904 into the receptive, manicured hands of Cleveland Democrats. Those gentlemen, reviving strict-construction as the guiding spirit of the Democratic platform, made much of Roosevelt's alleged infringements of the Constitution. They could not have chosen a more ineffectual, inopportune issue. Roosevelt took special pride in asserting and extending the power of the federal government. Only by so doing had he been able to effect his policies. When the Democrats pronounced him constitutionally unscrupulous, Main Street, if it listened at all, preferred to recollect his forays against intractable finance.

So also in foreign policy Roosevelt attained two goals. The principles he forcibly reiterated long before his administration clearly foreshadowed his every action in matters international, but his actions incidentally had political value, partly because of the manner in which he publicized them. If he privately suspected this, even if such a suspicion subconsciously influenced his decisions, he took into account in his dealing with foreign powers only the international ramifications of what he did. The record is long. Believing as he did in the responsibilities of conquest and imperialism, he defied the sugar lobby, the Democrats, and a considerable fraction of Republicans to obtain for Cuba a tariff advantage essential for the economic stability of the government he had helped to establish there; regrettably he incurred the opposition of both professional pro- and anti-Catholics during his long negotiations with the Vatican about the disposition of the friars' lands in the Philippines. Buttressing his views on the Monroe Doctrine, the inviolability of territories held by the United States, and the strategic importance of the Caribbean and especially of an isthmian canal, he warned the Kaiser to stay clear of Venezuela (though Roosevelt's diplomatic interposition in 1902 and 1903 was not as threatening as he later recalled); he intervened in the troubled financial affairs of Santo Domingo; he thought he risked war — though he only offended a friend — by refusing to yield to Canada either a jot of diplomatic grace or a tittle of the disputed Alaskan boundary; and he "took Panama," boldly, self-righteously, for some good reasons but for no compelling ones, withal outrageously. In the interests of peace — which, when attended by honor, he cultivated — and for the sake of stability in the ominous disequilibrium of the Orient, he interceded successfully to terminate war between Russia and Japan. Peace had profited earlier by his willingness to let the Venezuelan debt be arbitrated and by the treaties of arbitration which he negotiated.

These were large achievements. They were also markedly opportune. In one administration Roosevelt had struck blows for peace, magnanimously assisted the victims of centuries of Spanish oppression in both hemispheres, twisted the lion's tail, planted Old Glory in new outposts, nourished it elsewhere, and presumably defied the strutting prince of Wilhelmstrasse whose fleet so recently had dared to embarrass Dewey's at Manila. To swell this significant account, Roosevelt for the sake of humanity and the New York vote nudged his reluctant Secretary of State to pray diplomatically to the Czar for leniency toward the persecuted Jews of Russia and Rumania. The complaints of the anti-imperialists might tarnish but they could not dent his record. About it any Republican campaigner, selecting his data to suit his district, could make, if he wished, an oration whose periods might caress wonderful substances of proved popularity. The Democrats wisely, except among the politically insignificant intellectuals of the East, made very little of foreign policy in 1904. They had no choice. Roosevelt had straddled that field.

By June 1904 when the Republican National Convention met, Roosevelt had made the organization on the floor his own and the rank and file his devoted gallery. Because Hanna had refused open combat, the President's patronage raids had not disrupted the party. Because Roosevelt's policies, however radically presented, were none the less acceptable to viable conservative minds, neither the President's executive actions nor his legislative program had alienated the party's stalwarts. Although they would soon resist further changes, they had in 1904 no serious grievances. The Grand Old Party stood solidly behind its grand new leader. Particularly since the Democracy, facing right, chose as its candidate the colorless New York judge, Alton B. Parker, Roosevelt, as the quadrennial carnival began, had every advantage.

Nevertheless, with a characteristic lack of confidence, Roosevelt worried. Even while his managers — disregarding his instructions — collected large funds from financiers who preferred any Republican to any Democrat, the President feared that Wall Street might buy the election for his opponents. He also feared that Tammany Hall and its lesser Democratic equivalents would bully successfully where they could not buy. This was all extremely unlikely, but Roosevelt was determined to be sure. To the campaign, therefore, he gave continuously his aggressive personal touch.

The Square Deal, during the campaign, laid upon the national table aces and trumps for various splinter groups. Releasing copies of his letters through the Associated Press, Roosevelt in 1904 wrote the officers of the Grand Army, the Society of the Army of the Cumberland, and the Veterans of Foreign Service, extending his "good wishes" and recounting their "exceptional record" which held "the respect and admiration" of their countrymen. Pension Order 78, issued with the President's approval in March and emphasized enthusiastically by Republican orators thereafter, made senescence alone qualification for a pension and lowered the ages of eligibility. Organized religion received attention comparable to that tendered the veterans. "I have been told that there is a little lukewarmness among the Methodists . . . ," Roosevelt informed the chairman of the national committee. "Cannot they be got at? . . . There are many hundreds of Methodist preachers in New York, and of course the Methodist laymen are a vitally important element in the party. The Rev. Ezra Tipple, . . . General Secretary of the Methodist Conference . . . is a great friend of ours. I think if you sent for him it would be a mighty good thing to do." To an influential New York Catholic, Roosevelt expressed his belief that there might someday be a Roman Catholic President. In 1884, he recalled, he had himself worked briefly to such an end. And, he reminded his correspondent, "in my social relations . . . the fact that such good friends of mine as Grant La Farge and Gussie Montant are Catholics never enters my head from one year's end to another." Perhaps 1904 was the exceptional year. In any case, bowing his head to his political relations, Roosevelt had seen to it that his appointments included Catholics as well as Methodists, Jews, Negroes, and leaders of labor.

Before his nomination the President began wooing the hyphen. In 1902 he had asked special recognition for Hungarian-Americans in New York. If German-Americans had resented the

Venezuelan episode, they had applauded Roosevelt's grand reception of Prince Henry of Prussia. In 1903 Roosevelt called the attention of the federal authorities at Ellis Island to the propriety of consulting Jewish-Americans, German-Americans, and Italian-Americans about the treatment of newly arrived immigrants. The hyphen in 1904 won further, timely notice. "I want you particularly to see Dr. Formaneck," Roosevelt, in a typical letter, instructed the secretary of the national committee. "I feel he could be of immense assistance among the Bohemians, perhaps especially in Illinois, but also elsewhere through the country." "Colonel Edward G. Halle has been one of our most vigorous and successful workers," the President wrote the Indiana Republican National Committeeman. "He knows the voter of German birth or antecedents as few other men know him . . . I do not think we can afford to take any chances in Indiana; and Colonel Halle can do remarkable work with the Germans."

Within doubtful states Roosevelt continued the work already begun to strengthen the Republican party. He attempted without success to unite the Maryland factions. In Delaware, on the advice of Postmaster General Payne, he directed a large share of national patronage to the faction of the incorrigible John E. Addicks who was then trying, vote by vote, to purchase the state. Much as he disliked Addicks' unsubtle methods, Roosevelt preferred, in a campaign year, a conscienceless Republican hegemony to a Democratic victory that might swell the power of the party which, he was sure, had perfected rascality. In Illinois the President courted amity by recognizing some demands of every factional leader. He would like to have made the state even more secure by arranging the nomination for Vice-President of Illinois' favorite son for that position. But enough of the Old Guard perversely insisted on a display of independence to effect the nomination of Senator Charles Fairbanks of Indiana. Since Indiana, like Illinois, was a faction-ridden state, Roosevelt had no objections to the standpat Fairbanks, a bland mediocrity popular in his own constituency.

Matters of principle made party conditions in Missouri and Wisconsin more difficult problems. In Missouri, Joseph Folk, a vigorous devotee of clean government, was assured of the Democratic gubernatorial nomination. Since it was "unlikely that any man we could nominate would be able to make headway in a fight against Folk . . . [who] stands in a pre-eminent degree for those principles . . . which underlie all good citizenship . . . ," Roosevelt suggested that the Republicans endorse Folk's nomination. But the party chose an undistinguished candidate of its own. The President would not endorse him, nor would he endanger the party by endorsing Folk. He preserved therefore a studied neutrality that satisfied at once his conscience and his partisanship. Folk won the governorship, but in the other state-wide contests, including those for Presidential electors, the Republicans prevailed in Missouri. In Wisconsin Robert M. La Follette's revolt against the stalwarts was ebullient in 1904. The party offered two tickets, each faction claiming legality for its own. Because Roosevelt valued the coöperation of both, he left Wisconsin alone until the state supreme court in October declared that La Follette's ticket was the legal one. At once Roosevelt instructed the national chairman to tell the stalwarts to fall in line. This they did not do, but according to a tacit division of labor they concentrated on congressional offices while La Follette took care of the state campaign. That arrangement made Wisconsin safe for the Republicans.

About New York Roosevelt worried most intensely. He considered its large electoral vote essential; his pride demanded that he carry his native state. But while the nomination of Judge Parker, also a New Yorker, united the Democrats in the state, the continuing tensions between Platt and Odell and between them both and the President's third force impaired Republican efficiency. In November 1903 Roosevelt summoned Platt and Odell to Washington where they all agreed "that Platt should be leader, but that Odell should have the management of the details . . ." Odell, reviving his attacks on the aging Platt, soon violated the truce. "Akela has lost his teeth and his spring," Roosevelt observed, "and the new leader of the pack wished to worry him to death in the open with everybody looking on." But "fortunately there were several Mowglis who were able to persuade both combatants that a less tempestuous course was advisable." Again, however, the peace proved to be but an armistice. And as the wolves resumed their snapping, the Democrats began to make much of "Odellism," charging the governor with using his dual power as chief executive and chairman of the state committee to create a personal dictatorship favorable to Manhattan's plutocracy.

The time had come for the third force to take over the state. If Odell were renominated or if he dictated the choice of his successor, "Odellism" could be a dangerous issue. Platt offered as an alternative only his Brooklyn vassal, whose chief assets were his celebrated "high-colored" waistcoats. A victory for either faction promised only immediate and continuing trouble. Roosevelt therefore, seeking a strong candidate of his own choosing, first urged Elihu Root to run. Long an active regular, renowned locally for his large talents, Root could easily have won both the nomination and the election. Moreover, Roosevelt predicted to Root, "if you ran for Governor and were elected, you would become the man most likely to be nominated by the Republicans for the Presidency in 1908 . . ." But Root refused. He considered himself too old; perhaps he also preferred offices less encumbered by institutional commitments. Roosevelt turned next to Nicholas Murray Butler, whom Odell was also willing to support. The Republican National Chairman and Root, the President wrote Butler, "are red-hot to have you run for Governor." Butler, however, also declined. He considered the presidency of Columbia University more desirable than a political position. Neither the great nor, apparently, the pompously near-great would accept the office that Roosevelt in 1898 had pursued with frenetic desire. The President therefore lowered his sights, focusing them on the lieutenant governor whose demonstrated loyalty to Roosevelt balanced his demonstrably limited capacities. The Collector of the Port made the President's choice known to an obedient convention. Acknowledging the inevitable gracefully, Platt's candidate withdrew. Unable to battle both the Platt and the Roosevelt factions, Odell then joined them. The directed nomination made the Republican ticket in New York rather less than distinguished, but it was clearly the President's ticket, and as the party arranged its campaign, Roosevelt seemed to run for governor as well as for his own election. Even in tandem he ran swiftly.

Although Roosevelt was the director-general of the campaign of 1904, he had to depend, as does any candidate, on a multitude of subordinates. These included, first of all, the men he had appointed to office or adopted from Hanna's organization. A second, equally useful group were the Republican congressional candidates whose personal campaigns could contribute locally to the party's appeal even as they drew strength from the President's national canvass. Of these campaigners the most important were the congressional veterans, for the most part standpatters, politicians who had superbly equipped personal organizations. Roosevelt had deferred to their requests for patronage. He carefully subscribed also to their policy on the protective tariff, the issue which had long commanded the extraordinary devotion of the Republican Old Guard. His advocacy of Cuban reciprocity, the President arranged, was to be considered in 1904 only an aberrant episode. Elihu Root, the administration's spokesman at the Republican National Convention, planned to tell the delegates that "the tariff will presently need revision." Roosevelt advised him to declare instead that "the tariff *may* presently need revision and if so should receive it at the hands of the friends and not the enemies of the protective system." This modification the platform incorporated. During the campaign Roosevelt chastised his Secretary of War for talking too glibly of tariff revision. He took care himself to express his general satisfaction with the high schedules of the Dingley Act, the party's obtaining instrument of protection.

For his chief of staff, the chairman of the Republican National Committee, Roosevelt selected George Bruce Cortelyou.* This was a wise decision. Cortelyou had been McKinley's personal secretary. He remained in his post under Roosevelt until 1903 when the President made him Secretary of Commerce and Labor. Informed about the party, acquainted with the agents of both his employers, trusted by businessmen, dependable, ambitious, urbane — indeed almost slick — Cortelyou possessed admirable qualifications for the chairmanship which Roosevelt procured for him. A few of the Old Guard accepted him resentfully, but on the whole the party was satisfied. So were the potential contributors to the campaign fund. Judge Parker tried to make an issue of "Cortelyouism," accusing the Republican chairman of blackmailing businessmen by threatening to publish the findings of the Bureau of Corporations. Cortelyou had no need for blackmail. The national chairman, the financial manager of the campaign, and the secretary of the national committee — formerly Hanna's secretary — simply continued to draw upon the replete accounts which Hanna in 1896 and 1900 had opened for the party. Parker's accusations, incapable of substantiation, served best to permit Roosevelt to make an indignant public denial.

No one had to fabricate an issue in 1904. The very live issue was Theodore Roosevelt. He would not have wanted it to be anything else, nor, if he had desired, could he have made it anything else. Unchangeable Democrats voted Democratic; unchangeable Republicans voted Republican; the less regular electorate made up its mind pretty much for or against Teddy. The organization secure, the party buttressed, and that issue defined, Roosevelt could have faced election with equanimity. Instead he persisted in viewing things as doubtful, finding solace

---

* Henry Clay Payne, who died in October 1904, was too ill to be considered for national chairman. Otherwise he would have qualified admirably.

in the conviction he had stated for the people that "if elected I shall go into the Presidency unhampered by any pledge, promise, or understanding . . . save my promise . . . that so far as in my power lies I shall see to it that every man has a square deal." He had also, of course, stacked the cards.

"I had no idea," Roosevelt admitted after the returns were in, "that there would be such a sweep." "I am stunned," he confided to his son Kermit, "by the overwhelming victory we have won. I had no conception that such a thing was possible . . . this was the day of greatest triumph I ever have had or ever could have, and I was very proud and happy." In the pleasant glow of success Roosevelt privately reconstructed his achievement: "Of course it would be foolish for me to say that I did not think that I myself was responsible for part of the victory. I have done a great deal of substantive work. I have never sought trouble, but I have never feared to take the initiative . . . I have had as staunch and able friends and supporters as ever a President had . . . Moreover, it is a peculiar gratification to me to have owed my election not to the politicians primarily, although of course I have done my best to get on with them; not to the financiers, although I have staunchly upheld the rights of property; but above all to Abraham Lincoln's 'plain people'; to the folk who work hard on farm, in shop, or on the railroads, or who own little stores, little businesses which they manage themselves."

This was perhaps an incorrectly weighted assessment. Before and during 1908 Roosevelt would, as he had before and during 1904, calculate and with exactitude adjust the necessary tensions of the political machinery he so nicely understood. Yet in 1908 he worked for another, for on election night in 1904 he renounced all intention of seeking renomination. He had won his kingdom. Now he would seek only his glory. And in both 1904 and 1908, because the "plain people" were always in his thoughts, because, as he told a correspondent, "I would literally, not figuratively, rather cut off my right hand than forfeit by any improper act of mine the trust and regard of these people," Roosevelt's calculations had more than an operational value. He took it upon himself to be the steward of the people, to interpret his trust. He had an aristocrat's confidence, however misplaced it may have been, in the validity of his own interpretations; he had no confidence in the interpretations of either a Bryan, a Parker, or a Hanna.

Roosevelt and Mark Hanna were both political pragmatists and both intelligent conservatives. Yet Roosevelt sensed, probably accurately, that more consciously than Hanna he was a moralist. He made his calculations to hold the power which, he felt, no possible rival knew how to use better than did he. Less self-assured men ordinarily make either poorer candidates or weaker Presidents.

The political system which Roosevelt managed so well had institutionalized long before he accepted its dimensions as the boundaries of his behavior. In controlling that system rather than attacking it he demonstrated during his first administration his perfection of the devices of party politics. He was emphatically professional. More than that, he delighted in his role. He had a simply wonderful time making the political puppets jump. He enjoyed power; he enjoyed making things work. These characteristics, by no means pertinent exclusively to politicians of any one party or any one creed, perhaps best become those who are preoccupied not so much with schematic principles as with operations and operating policies.

This was the case with Roosevelt. His Square Deal defied systematic conceptualization because it was unsystematic. He did not sell the electorate either a panacea, an idea, or an elaborated theory of political economy. Rather, with surpassing vitality, he persuaded the voters that he had a conscience and would be fair. This distinguished Roosevelt alike from Hanna, who persuaded "plain people" impersonally if at all, and from Bryan, who usually attached his picturesque personality to some graphic program. In trying to be fair, moreover, Roosevelt did indeed do "a great deal of substantive work." And particularly

after he won the Presidency in his own right, he used his power
to translate his conscience into policies. His purpose had in itself
a structure of which he became more and more conscious. It remains to be seen how he brought Congress to make his purpose
law. It remains also to examine, against the needs of an industrialized society that in his time recognized the necessity for
change, the large meaning of his purpose.

Chapter VI

PRESIDENT, CONGRESS, AND CONTROL

At no time was Theodore Roosevelt more intent on achievement, more attuned to opinion, or more conscious of the nice relationships within his party than in November 1904 when he had at last become President in his own right. "Stunned" though he may have been "by the overwhelming victory" he had won, he nevertheless turned at once to fashion a program for Congress. His pursuit of the objective in that program he most valued — a measure to regulate the railroads — demonstrated perhaps better than any other episode in his Presidency both his facility in dealing with Congress and his mature evaluation of the kind of public arrangement which would best permit necessary government control over industrial operations.

Roosevelt was never a speculative man. Thinking as he did primarily about specific issues, he understood and judged large problems in terms of their more limited parts. By his intent, furthermore, his actions spoke for him better than did his words. He made his points most convincingly when he dealt with situations instead of theories. His talents and his purpose are best understood, therefore, by examination of those activities he counted most significant. This was the importance of his railroad program. For it he exercised those qualities of executive leadership upon which successful Presidents must depend; with it he expected to provide the devices upon which the governing of an industrial society might depend.

On various occasions Roosevelt overcame the obstacles imposed by the American Constitution and party system. Again and again he arranged that his recommendations should embody or win the concern of party leaders who, reflecting conflicting regional and economic demands, often had little in common other than the desire to retain office. He maneuvered legislation past the gamut of committee hearings and congressional debates where powerful chairmen and adroit parliamentarians knew how to delay and divert, sometimes defeat, the consensus of the party. Prepared as he was to influence his party and Congress by mobilizing public opinion, careful as he was never to press his program beyond the limits he calculated as practicable, he nurtured bills for the inspection of meat-packing, for the definition and enforcement of pure food and drug standards, for the expansion of the navy. But of all the legislation Roosevelt proposed, he had to work hardest and most skillfully for his railroad program.

Conspicuous inequities in American industrial life drew Roosevelt's concentration to railroad regulation. Existing laws had failed to affect the practices by which railway managers, usually unwillingly, often solely to protect their properties, favored the largest, most ruthless industrial corporations. Faced, as they were, with enormous fixed costs — interest on huge bonded debts, depreciation on large and expensive equipment — railroads, to insure enough business to meet their overheads, acceded to the demands of such corporations as the Standard Oil Company, the Armour Company, and the American Sugar Refining Company for freight rates below those accorded to smaller shippers. Although the Elkins Act of 1903 forbade these discriminations, the law was continually violated outright. These violations the offenders could usually obscure by bookkeeping methods over which the Interstate Commerce Commission had no control. The Elkins Act, furthermore, was continually circumvented. Standard Oil and Armour, among many others, besides seeking rebates, obtained discriminatory favor by arranging to receive inordinately large fees from railroads for the use of private cars

— such as oil or refrigerator cars — and private sidings and terminals which the corporations owned. Practices such as these helped large shippers to grow wealthier, to absorb their less-favored competitors, to increase thereby their control over markets, and consequently to set prices for their products higher than those that might otherwise have obtained. If the railroads suffered, they too often compensated for their losses by establishing seemingly excessive freight rates either on commodities — like grain and carbon black — whose producers were in no position to demand favors, or over routes where there was no competition for transportation services.

Determined to remedy these conditions, Roosevelt proposed that Congress give the Interstate Commerce Commission effective power over railroad accounts, over private railway equipment, and — most important — in modest degree, over railroad rates. To translate this recommendation into legislation, Roosevelt first created a controlled environment within his party and then adapted his views to parliamentary conditions. He established by his tactics a productive relationship between the executive and Congress. While his program was debated in the Senate, in the session of 1905–1906, Roosevelt defined explicitly the concepts of executive control essential to his more elaborate theses on political economy. During and immediately after the lame duck session of 1904–1905, by strategy as revealing of his purpose as was his later, more explicit definition, he committed the Republicans to railroad regulation and twice got through the House bills that embodied his policy.

✤

Roosevelt's first negotiation necessitated the sacrifice of his announced intention to direct a revision of the tariff. It depended, however, on the continuing threat of tariff revision. The manner in which Roosevelt used tariff revision to advance railroad regulation and the reasons for which he subordinated the one issue to the other have meaning both as a revelatory instance of executive leadership and as an important indication of the central purpose of Roosevelt's political action.

Only two days after the election of 1904 Roosevelt informed Nicholas Murray Butler that he had "already begun the effort to secure a bill to revise and reduce the tariff." The President well understood the dimensions of this task. In his first term he had almost lost to the Republican standpatters his prolonged fight for reciprocity with Cuba. Yet even as his second term began he raised the whole tariff issue, because, he suggested in a heated moment, "we beat the Democrats on the issue that protection was robbery, and that when necessary we would amend or revise the tariff ourselves." This explanation, as Roosevelt knew, did violence to the facts. If the Republicans had any effective national issue in the campaign of 1904 other than Theodore Roosevelt and the Square Deal, it was certainly not tariff revision. The President had accepted a platform that complacently praised Dingleyism; he had strongly endorsed the principle of protection, chastised his Secretary of War for favoring tariff reduction in a campaign speech, and denounced the Democrats for their insistence that protection was robbery.

In his more candid and quiet moments, Roosevelt explained his position with less hyperbole and more effect. "I am convinced," he wrote, "that there is, among the good Republicans and among the masses of independent Democrats who supported us . . . , a very strong feeling in favor of what I prefer to call an amendment rather than a revision of the tariff laws." "My own judgment," Roosevelt confessed, "is that it is dangerous to undertake to do anything, but that it is fatal not to undertake it . . ."

This assessment of political sentiment had some validity. The Republican differences on the tariff were major and real. A considerable minority, primarily composed of Western agrarians, favored a general reduction of schedules. Others, for the most part representing Minnesota and Massachusetts shoe, woolens, and flour manufacturers, advocated reciprocity agreements, particularly with Canada, under which their constituents would benefit by cheaper raw materials and larger export markets. These revisionists contended that the party had promised the voters adjustment, though not abandonment, of the protective system. Failing this, they warned, the Democrats, as they had in Massachusetts in 1904, would profitably exploit the tariff issue. They urged Roosevelt, therefore, to summon an extra session of Congress to deal with the tariff, preferably in the spring of 1905. Most Republican leaders, including the most powerful members of Congress, however, opposing any changes in the tariff and jealously guarding the principle of protection, asserted that the election returns evidenced popular satisfaction with the Dingley rates.

Sympathetic to the revisionists, Roosevelt also recognized their strength, but he lacked their conviction and, conscious of the greater strength of their opposition, he feared the divisive hostilities and probable futility that characteristically attended tariff debates. For him the tariff was a matter of expediency. Never willing to risk a division of his party that would endanger his favored measures on an issue about which he did not feel strongly, Roosevelt, in spite of his occasional hyperbole, approached revision with consummate caution. Yet because of the articulate minority support for revision, Roosevelt seized upon tariff discussions as a useful weapon. The prospect of revision, even of a tariff debate, alarmed the standpatters sufficiently to provide an effective disciplinary tool. For Presidential coöperation on the tariff, they were ultimately willing to reach an understanding with Roosevelt, perhaps even to strike a bargain, on railroad regulation.

To that end Roosevelt maneuvered skillfully. His problem was to talk of tariff revision firmly enough to frighten the Old Guard but gently enough not to alienate them. If in the process of negotiation and legislation he could arrange tariff modifications, the achievement would be welcome, but he considered it always incidental. From the very beginning the form of his tariff negotiations suggested that they were less an objective than a device.

Roosevelt did not demand; he consulted. "When I see you," he informed the Republican whip in the House, "I want to take up the question of the tariff . . . It seems to me that our party ought to revise the tariff now, but of course I do not want to say anything about it unless the leaders of the House approve, because I realize thoroughly that the matter is primarily one for you all in the House." A week later he added that "an extra session, even if it was not held until the 1st of September [1905], would be most desirable," for, he feared, "if we wait until the regular session, . . . the Democrats will talk the matter over for a year and then we shall be swamped at the Congressional elections." Yet he acknowledged to one senator that "there should be only a few and moderate changes"; and even as he labeled protection "robbery," he assured the president of the American Iron and Steel Institute that he intended "of course, to abide by the general judgment of the party." Meanwhile Roosevelt's personal secretary had announced on November 19 that the President's forthcoming State of the Union message would not mention the tariff.

Clearly Roosevelt never considered the tariff worth a fight. Three weeks after telling Butler he had begun his "effort to secure" a revision, he confessed privately that the issue was practically dead. "The trouble," he explained, "is that there are large parts of the country which want no tariff revision, and of course their representatives are hostile to any agitation of the subject. They say, with entire truth, that neither in the platform nor in any communication of mine is there any promise whatever that there shall be tariff revision. They also say, with equal truth, that the tariff changes should not be great, and that those clamoring for tariff changes are certainly to be disappointed at whatever is done . . . I am going to make every effort to get something of what I desire . . . ; but I shall not split with my party on the matter . . ." Having shed all pretense that the party had a mandate for revision, Roosevelt several days later, again privately, admitted that he had no intention of tackling the tariff in the immediate future. "At present, . . ." he wrote Butler, "there is a strong majority against [amendment or reduction] . . . The minority . . . is entirely split up as to the articles on which the amendment should come . . . This means that unless circumstances change in the next sixty days it will be . . . worse than idle to call the extra session early."

It was not that Roosevelt had retreated. He had never really attacked. But before making his candid admissions to Butler, he had, with less candor, begun to bargain. Just before leaving Illinois for Washington, that archpriest of protection, Speaker of the House Joe Cannon, had received from Roosevelt a disturbing draft, dated November 30, of a special message on the tariff that the President proposed sending to Congress. "While it is above all things desirable that the present tariff law should be kept in its essence unchanged," the draft read, "there may well be certain points as to which it can be amended. There may be some schedules that . . . should be changed . . . If it were possible to provide for reciprocity by a maximum and minimum scale to be applied in the discretion of the Executive, this should be done . . . In any event some of the schedules should now be examined . . ." If these modest proposals could not alarm the Speaker, they were certain at least to worry him. Carefully Roosevelt mitigated even worry, observing that he sent the draft "merely for the sake of having something which can be worked out, after you have consulted the men fresh from the people . . ."

Roosevelt timed the dispatch of the draft nicely. The Speaker was not to be allowed to forget that the tariff issue remained, even though the annual message, opening the last session of the Fifty-eighth Congress, said nothing of revision. He could not be allowed to forget, for that message voiced aggressively Roosevelt's demand for railroad regulation. "The government," Roosevelt instructed Congress, "must in increasing degree supervise and regulate the workings of the railways engaged in interstate commerce; and such increased supervision is the only alternative to an increase of the present evils on the one hand or a still more radical policy on the other. In my judgment, the most important legislative act now needed as regards the regulation of corporations is this act to confer on the Interstate Commerce Commission the power to revise rates and regulations."

With these words Roosevelt set off the battle over railroad regulation. On this issue the party was as divided as on the tariff. And the division, to Roosevelt's advantage, followed similar personal and sectional lines. The advocates of revision and reciprocity were also the proponents of regulation. Speaking for Western agrarians and grain dealers and for Massachusetts manufacturers, they wanted federal review of freight rates which had been, from their point of view, increasingly discriminatory. On the other hand, the standpatters, speaking either for or with the big business interests, had long resisted any departures from nineteenth-century *laissez faire*.

For the railroad program, to which there was strong Republican opposition, Roosevelt had genuine concern. He consulted Congress less and demanded more. It was "unwise and unsafe from every standpoint," he had concluded, "to fail to give the Interstate Commerce Commission additional power of an effective kind in regulating . . . rates." This, he believed, was an essential ingredient for his basic determination "that the Government should effectively shape the policy [of the] . . . Square Deal."

Thus fervently committed, but confronting a powerful opposition, Roosevelt capitalized on the divisions in Congress produced by regional and economic self-interest. The low-tariff, antirailroad group was to have one reform, the high-tariff, prorailroad group to hold one redoubt. Saving what he considered vital by sacrificing what he considered marginal, Roosevelt for the sake of railroad regulation jettisoned the draft of the special message on the tariff that had worried Cannon.

Toward this decision Cannon, by his own account, exercised his influence. The Speaker, and perhaps also Senator Nelson Aldrich, may have struck a bargain with Roosevelt on railroad regulation. The circumstantial evidence that there was some bargain or understanding is overwhelming. The alignments of economic self-interest provided fertile ground which Roosevelt had cultivated for such an understanding. The diminuendo in Roosevelt's private letters to Butler on tariff revision suggests that the President had settled his course in early December. Roosevelt's tariff conferences continued through the first week of January when, according to Cannon's account, he told the congressional leaders that revision would await the election of his successor. Cannon exaggerated, but shortly after that conference Roosevelt defined his position to a friend. "I am having anything but a harmonious time about the tariff and about the interstate commerce . . . ," he wrote. "On the interstate commerce business, which I regard as a matter of principle, I shall fight. On the tariff, which I regard as a matter of expediency, I shall endeavor to get the best results I can, but I shall not break with my party." And for the time being, with regard to the tariff, Cannon and the party were one. Two days later Roosevelt wrote Cannon: "Stop in here as soon as you can. I care very little for what the newspapers get in the way of passing sensationalism; but I do not want the people of the country to get the idea that there will be any split or clash between you and me on the tariff or anything else."

Roosevelt permitted no clash. He made no recommendation for specific or general revisions. Although he encouraged efforts for reciprocity arrangements with Canada and Newfoundland, he gave those efforts only desultory support in his dealings with Congress. At the other end of Pennsylvania Avenue, Cannon gave railroad legislation a clear track. The Speaker, it has been argued, saw to it that no bill passed until so late in the session that the Senate could not act. Actually Cannon had no need for such a scheme. The hearings of the House Committee on Interstate Commerce, as much as the debates on the floor, delayed approval of the bill. When it did finally come to a vote, it passed with a decisive majority of 309. Had it passed earlier, judging by the course of the railroad bill at the following session, it would have failed to get through the Senate before adjournment. And during the following sessions Cannon again presented no obstacles to railway regulation.

In the months following the expiration of the Fifty-eighth Congress, Roosevelt continued to rely on the threat of tariff revision. During that Congress the Senate Committee on Interstate Commerce began to hold hearings that continued through most of May 1905. Railroad executives, mobilized by Samuel Spencer, the chief of J. P. Morgan's railway division, and encouraged by sympathetic senators, used these hearings as a sounding board for opposition to Roosevelt. Outside of the committee room the railroads underwrote an expensive publicity campaign in which various business organizations, including the National Association of Manufacturers, came to their aid. With increasing fervor they rehearsed the dangerous folly of the President's proposals. As this propaganda received wide dissemination in the press, the enemies of regulation seemed to be gaining an upper hand.

Yet Roosevelt in this period displayed a measured optimism. Perhaps he suspected that the railroads would, as they did, overreach themselves. Doubtless he foresaw that investigations of the Standard Oil Company and the beef trust then under way would furnish much evidence to sustain him. Surely he had confidence that his speeches and those of his advisers would counteract the railroad propaganda. The President was continually at the hustings. In the winter at the Philadelphia Union League Club, later in Texas and Colorado, at Chautauqua and Chicago, along the southeastern seaboard, he spoke to adulating audiences of the righteousness, and yet the reasonableness, of his cause. If, in part, the prestige of his office drew them to hear him, the fervor in his falsetto persuaded them to listen. The overdrawn counterpropaganda of the railroads, whatever its merit in logic, could scarcely compete in a society primed by the muckrakers with the explosive personality of the President. Assertively he equated his view of rate-making with his then regnant dictum of a square deal for every man. He would restrain the perverters of privilege who by their manipulations of rates and rebates purloined the just profits of their honest competitors and threatened to provoke by their excesses the menace of socialism. This was a crisis (Theodore Roosevelt coped constantly with crises), but he would shackle greed and, routing the proponents of nationalization, save the railroads from themselves.

But Roosevelt did not confine his energies to the podium. In May he reminded the Old Guard that the tariff could still be an issue. To emphasize the tariff-railroad understanding that the battle of propaganda might otherwise have obscured, Roosevelt thrust at the standpatters' most sensitive spot. One guardian of protection had admitted the previous fall that the "strongest argument" for revision was that American manufacturers sold goods in foreign markets for less than they received at home. This condition, he then pointed out, while perhaps inequitable, was irremediable, for "no revision of the tariff which still left a protective margin could prevent" it. To challenge the differential in the export and domestic prices of protected commodities was to challenge the whole principle of protection. This was precisely what Roosevelt did.

On May 16, 1905, while the railroad propaganda was at its peak, an announcement that the Isthmian Canal Commission had decided to purchase supplies for the construction of the canal in foreign markets immediately staggered the standpatters. They were further shocked when Roosevelt flatly assumed all responsibility for the adoption of this "cheapest-market" policy. The New York *Times* called the announcement the "doom of Dingleyism." The steel industry's most active lobbyist and his reliable congressional echoes shared the view of the New York *Press* that the cheapest-market policy, repudiating the high-tariff mandate of 1904, was "a faithless service of outrage." The president of the National Association of Manufacturers and the secretary of the American Protective Tariff Association tersely labeled Roosevelt's action "un-American."

Less emotional observers noted that Roosevelt probably intended not to abandon protection but to call the attention of Congress to the whole subject of tariff adjustment. They were correct, for after succeeding admirably in just that, the President was satisfied. Three days after the announcement was made, Cannon conferred with Secretary of War Taft, who then rescinded the cheapest-market order, referring to the next Congress the question of canal purchases. Responsible, according to his own statement, for the order, Roosevelt must also have been responsible for the reversal.

The dramatic episode of the canal purchases served as Roosevelt's most forceful but not as his final reminder to the standpatters that the tariff remained a potential issue. In August, White House "leaks" inspired newspaper reports that the President contemplated calling an extra session of Congress to consider tariff revision. If he did not plant these rumors, Roosevelt at least used them. To his Secretary of the Treasury, an uncompromising protectionist, he wrote in the tone he had long used: "I entirely agree with all you say as to the dangers which accompany tariff revision — or any attempt at it, but as yet I am not sure whether there are not at least equal dangers in avoiding [it] . . . I want to go over the entire matter very carefully with all of the Congressional leaders before we decide which set of risks to take." Roosevelt quickly decided. It was scarcely necessary for him to consult his congressional leaders — they had understood each other for months. In mid-August, Taft, then in the Philippines, released a message from the President that there would be no extra session of Congress. The regular session, Roosevelt had already implied at Chautauqua and stated in private, would be, insofar as he could control it, devoted to rate regulation.

In December 1905, the Fifty-ninth Congress convened. During the fall, the campaigns in Massachusetts and Iowa had kept the tariff issue alive while Roosevelt, in the South, had focused on the railways. The President's annual message, silent, as it had been in 1904, on the tariff, made railroad regulation the central objective of the Administration. In the long struggle that ensued, the tariff once more provided a lever. In the House, a combination of Democrats and Administration Republicans passed a bill reducing the rates on Philippine products. Intended as an instrument of colonial policy, the measure was nevertheless considered by standpat Republicans to breach the principle of protection. Administration leaders in the Senate by their lassitude permitted it to die in committee while, like Roosevelt, they concentrated their energy and their power on the railroad bill. For this division of labor no explicit bargain need have been made, for all matters pertaining to the tariff continued in 1906 to be, as they had been since 1904, useful whips rather than real targets. By 1906 Roosevelt had abandoned all effort for tariff revision, yet essentially he abandoned only a bargaining instrument. At no time in his long public career did tariff revision much concern him. For eighteen months, however, he employed adroitly the specter of tariff agitation.

By defining tariff revision as a matter of expediency and railroad regulation as a matter of principle, Roosevelt established his own position. His life, he felt, was a quest for the moral. What he meant by morality was not always clear, but the concept had obvious components. In some cases, that which was moral was that which could be accomplished. Given two paper trusts to bust, Roosevelt had attacked the less offensive but legally vulnerable pool and ignored the more oppressive but legally secure holding company. By this criterion, railroad regulation was in 1904 more moral than tariff revision, for public and political opinion on the railways divided on nonpartisan lines and the Republican party was less committed to the Elkins Act as a line of defense than to the Dingley Act. That which was moral was also often that which was popular. In making a crucial test of the Sherman Antitrust Act, Roosevelt had prosecuted neither the largest nor the most monopolistic holding company. He had chosen, rather, a railroad merger that had been born of a discreditable stockmarket battle, that consisted of units long unpopular with shippers in the areas in which they ran, that had already been challenged by state authorities. Unlike Justice Holmes, Roosevelt wanted to bring the voice of the people to bear on decisions. Showered as they were in 1904 by private and official disclosures of the iniquities of rebates, the evils of Armour, the machinations of Standard Oil, most of the people, particularly middle-class people, were less interested in the tariff than in direct controls of big business, especially the railways.

But Roosevelt's morality was not simply opportunistic. He felt that the central issue of his time pivoted on the control of business because this control determined conduct, and morality was for him a matter of conduct. He feared not the size but the policies of big business. He cared not about profits but about the manner of earning profits. This was the essence of the Square Deal. Roosevelt fought for railroad regulation because it was designed to control process. By his standard, tariff schedules — static matters — were as unimportant as an administrative agency overseeing day-by-day business arrangements was essential.

These dimensions of morality — practicability, popularity, and especially preoccupation with process — characterized Roosevelt's emergent progressivism. They permitted him to yield, when necessary, on details in order to advance his favored measures. They also persuaded him for reasons of policy as well as of tactics to arrange the understanding on tariff revision and railroad regulation that prepared the way for perhaps the most significant legislation of his Presidency.

Railroad rates could not be regulated, however, until Roosevelt, having committed the House to his policy, slowly brought the Senate also into line. In that second task, as in the persuading of the House, he exercised artfully the resources of office and person by which a President can lead Congress, in spite of the separation of powers imposed by the Constitution, to consummate his policies. Roosevelt's impressive ability to work within the structure of government, like his facility in managing the party, depended less on his arresting manner than on his appreciation of the institutions that shaped American political life. Like Edmund Burke, perhaps the greatest of British conservatives, Roosevelt valued the long wash of historical development, sometimes controlled, sometimes accidental, that had given form to the political society in which he lived. Both were wisely careful never to set up a system of their own. Like Burke, Roosevelt delighted in the processes by which political achievement and further institutional development were made possible. Both considered political peace the breathing-time which gave them leisure further to contrive. As he guided his railroad program through the Senate where formidable obstacles blocked his way, Roosevelt needed and took his daily gladness in situations "of power and energy," in government — as Burke described it — "founded on compromise and barter."

•

Behind all the political manipulation, beneath all the legalistic forensics, the issue was control. Theodore Roosevelt intended that an administrative agency should have the authority to rectify the inequities in the business of transportation. Nelson Aldrich, the resourceful leader of the President's opposition, intended that it should not. Roosevelt demanded that the Interstate Commerce Commission be invested with power to revise railroad rates. Here, he felt, lay the key to control. Aldrich, when he drew his lines, sought to transfer the final decision on rates from the commission to the courts, to leave the judiciary in its traditional, ineffectual, disorderly role of monitor of the price of transportation. President and senator, sensitive always to each other's strength, delighting in the test, came slowly to a crisis.

"I am well aware," Roosevelt stated in his annual message to

Congress of 1905, "of the difficulties of the [railroad] legislation that I am suggesting, and of the need of temperate and cautious action in securing it. I should emphatically protest against improperly radical or hasty action . . . [But] the question of transportation lies at the root of all industrial success, and the revolution in transportation which has taken place during the last half-century has been the most important factor in the growth of the new industrial conditions . . . At present the railway is [the highway of commerce] . . . and we must do our best to see that it is kept open to all on equal terms . . . It is far better that it should be managed by private individuals than by the government. But it can only be so managed on condition that justice is done the public . . . What we need to do is to develop an orderly system, and such a system can only come through the gradually increased exercise of the right of efficient government control."

A year earlier Roosevelt had sent Congress only a paragraph on railroad legislation. Now he spelled out the elements of what he considered an orderly system of control. These he had derived from the accumulated findings of the Bureau of Corporations and the Interstate Commerce Commission and from the expert advice of the lawyers and railroad men in his Cabinet. Their recommendations, embodied in the Hepburn Bill with Administration guidance substantially as Roosevelt had announced them, covered every aspect of the railroad problem then recognized by the foremost authority on railroad economics in the United States. Grounded as it was on thorough study by essentially conservative men, much of Roosevelt's program provoked little congressional dissent.

The area of agreement was large. The Elkins Antirebate Act of 1903 had failed utterly to prevent the discriminations it explicitly forbade. Alive to this, and to the public's growing displeasure over the outrageous practices of Armour and Standard Oil, practices as harmful to the railroads as to the competitors of the favored, Congress shared the President's opinion that "all private-car lines, industrial roads, refrigerator charges, and the like should be expressly put under the supervision of the Interstate Commerce Commission . . ." Conscious of the experience of the government in investigating both railways and industrial concerns, Congress, like Roosevelt, had reached the commonsense conclusion that standardized records open to official inspection were a prerequisite for the determination of adequate policies of regulation as well as for the prevention of familiar abuses in corporation management. Congress was also willing, by providing for expeditious action in cases arising under the commerce act, to destroy "the weapon of delay, almost the most formidable weapon in the hands of those whose purpose is to violate the law." *

Had Roosevelt recommended and Congress agreed to nothing else, these provisions would in themselves have been worth-while but inadequate achievements. They did not fundamentally alter the existing relationship between the federal government and the railroads. They established no new device of regulation. The restriction of rebates, now strengthened, had earlier existed; the inspection of records, now facilitated, had long since begun; the expedition of trial for suits involving infractions of the Interstate Commerce Act had already been provided for suits arising under the Antitrust Act. Roosevelt's orderly system of efficient government control depended not on these precedents but on an innovation to which many in Congress were still openly hostile. The President proposed that the I.C.C. be given limited authority to make rates. As he carefully defined it, this was his central objective.

Roosevelt took his first and final position on rates in his annual message of 1904. He there considered it "undesirable . . . finally to clothe the commission with general authority to fix railroad rates." "As a fair security to shippers," however, he insisted that

---

* Without Presidential prodding, the Senate added to the Hepburn Bill two important clauses, one imposing criminal penalties for certain violations, another, more significant, forbidding corporations producing such commodities as coal from owning the railroads that transported them.

"the commission should be vested with the power, where a given rate has been challenged and after full hearing found to be unreasonable, to decide, subject to judicial review, what shall be a reasonable rate to take its place; the ruling of the commission to take effect immediately." The "reasonable rate," Roosevelt implied by his reference to the Supreme Court's interpretation of the Interstate Commerce Act, was to be only a maximum rate. This meaning he made explicit in 1905 when he requested that the commission receive power "to prescribe the limit of rate beyond which it shall not be lawful to go — the maximum reasonable rate, as it is commonly called."

Roosevelt's Attorney General had advised that legislation empowering the commission to set definite rate schedules — the objective of many Democratic and some Western Republican senators — might be declared unconstitutional. "The one thing I do not want," Roosevelt explained to one critic, "is to have a law passed and then declared unconstitutional." Furthermore, he argued, the authority to prescribe a maximum rate, while perhaps short of the ultimate ideal, promised immediate, substantial improvement in existing conditions. "If the Commission has the power to make the maximum rate that which the railroad gives to the most favored shipper, it will speedily become impossible thus to favor any shipper . . ." If, after a test, it should prove inadequate, he would then be willing to try to secure a definite rate proposition. "I believe," he explained to the impatient, "in men who take the next step; not those who theorize about the two-hundredth step."

Roosevelt intended primarily to protect individual shippers from excessive or discriminatory rates. He agreed that the maximum rate provision would afford little remedy for discrimination between commodities or between localities, but such discriminations seemed to him relatively impersonal. He cared less about freight classification and long and short haul differentials because he could not readily associate those matters with a doer of evil and a victim. Discriminations against a small shipper or exorbitant rates the President understood and despised. They were, he was sure, immoral. His interest had also political meaning, for the spokesmen of the shippers' organizations concentrated on the problems that a maximum rate provision could begin to resolve. They neglected to mention, and Roosevelt did not apparently recognize, that no recommendation in the annual messages or provision in the Hepburn Bill prevented shippers or their consignees from passing on rate burdens originating in any discriminatory device to the still unorganized, essentially undiscerning consumers.

The maximum rate proposal, in many respects inadequate, properly labeled so by liberals of the time, nevertheless earned for Roosevelt the opprobrious criticism of a large part of the business community and the tenacious opposition of a near majority of the United States Senate. Modest as the proposal was, it challenged the most cherished prerogative of private management, the most hoary tenet of free private enterprise — the ability freely to make prices. This threat gave Roosevelt a reputation, persisting still among railway executives, of being a scandalous advocate of something closely akin to socialism. A more radical proposition, the President well knew, would have had no chance for success.

Roosevelt had constructed the Hepburn Bill with practiced care. Including as it did just enough to satisfy his purpose, it contained nothing that would alarm the marginal supporters without whom it could not survive. This was the last in a series of calculated tactics by which Roosevelt had prepared the parliamentary environment for his railroad program. "I have a very strong feeling," he acknowledged, "that it is a President's duty to get on with Congress if he possibly can, and that it is a reflection upon him if he and Congress come to a complete break." Avoiding a break, understanding his situation, he made the powers of his office and the talents of his person the instruments of viable leadership.

He had begun by trading tariff reform for railroad regulation.

He had continued, after the adjournment of the lame duck session of the Fifty-eighth Congress, by taking his railroad issue, then the foremost national political problem, to the people. At the hustings his vigorous pleading won enthusiastic acclaim. His "plain people," for the most part, heard only the voice of their champion. Significantly, however, more careful, more cautious listeners, disregarding his dramatic allusions, at once could ascertain the moderation of his demands. Roosevelt's message was simple. His demands were not new. Indeed, Roosevelt added nothing to the principles or to the histrionics of the Granger and Populist railroad regulators of years gone by. But he did bring to their long-rejected national program a new respectability, an incomparable personal vitality, and assurances, impressive to thoughtful conservatives, that he, unlike his predecessors, would direct regulation to constructive ends.

The last was particularly important. By the fall of 1905 such reliable Republican senators from the West as Allison of Iowa and Spooner of Wisconsin, traditionally conservators of the status quo, now sensitive to the growing complaints of the farmers and shippers whose protests had preceded and exceeded Roosevelt's, realized that their political life rested upon an unprecedented capitulation to their constituents. In the President they recognized a safe sponsor for reform. If his language seemed at times extravagant, if his central purpose was a genuine departure from the past, he nevertheless, they knew from experience, guarded their party and, in the largest sense, their principles. This knowledge may also have comforted others who deeply distrusted the emotions Roosevelt evoked. Before the Fifty-ninth Congress convened, the roar of the President's crowds penetrated, perhaps, the cold quiet where Nelson Aldrich, by preference undisturbed, made policy. That master of the Senate, in any case, was thereafter willing to make a conciliatory gesture toward Roosevelt and his allies.

The President had set his stage. Reminded of the arrangements by which the tariff remained inviolate, the new House in February 1906, with only seven adverse votes, passed the Hepburn Bill. It provided for every objective of the Administration. The most thoughtful member of the I.C.C., Commissioner Prouty, told Roosevelt that it represented "an advance so extraordinary that he had never dared to suppose it would be possible to pass it." The President judged that it was "as far as we could with wisdom go at this time." Politically he was surely correct. Although an aroused constituency cheered the champions of the bill in the Senate, Nelson Aldrich, as debate began, had yet to surrender command of the chamber he had so long dominated. Roosevelt, until this time the aggressor, had now to adjust to the strength and the tactics of a talented oppositionist.

How unlike the President in many ways his adversary was: so urbane, so controlled, so indifferent to manifestations of approval, so patently disdainful of the string-tie statesmanship surrounding him; but, like Roosevelt, so bemused by the endless adventure of governing men! Did his friend Allison have, of a summer, to explain himself in ponderous periods from a rural podium? How dreary for Allison. Aldrich preferred the politics that the caucus controlled, the constituents one met graciously over liqueurs, the measured exchanges between mutually respectful equals who understood the manners and the meaning of their power. For all that, Aldrich was not the less discerning, not the less tenacious. Many of the dreadful things that Theodore did, the senator knew, he had to do. The people, after all, could vote. The railroads were unpopular. Roosevelt could have his bill, but not the way he wanted it. A gesture now, a delaying action — then, perhaps, the worst would pass. Perhaps, again, it would not pass; the comfortable world was changing. In that case, delay had of itself some value. And the means to resist were familiar and strong.

Aldrich had a corps of allies: among the Republicans, the intractables, all reliable, some expert parliamentarians, some outstanding men. There were also among the Democrats those who regularly resisted any reform and others, bound by quixotic tradition confounded with visions of miscegenation, who could be made to shy at any extension of the federal executive power. These were less reliable. Yet Aldrich in the past by prestige and by persuasion had combined these parts into a solid phalanx to front, unbudging, the bills that carried change.

Aldrich, disingenuous, moved quietly to bring the Hepburn Bill with its objectionable clause on rates into the arena where he and his allies had long had their way. While the measure lay before the Committee on Interstate and Foreign Commerce he labored at a disadvantage. There, with few exceptions, his trusted assistants had no seat. There Roosevelt's friends, making the President's moderation their own, seemed capable by coöperation with the Democratic committeemen of carrying crucial votes. There Jonathan Dolliver, the junior senator from Iowa, then beginning the progressive period of his career, ably pleaded the case of the Administration. Dolliver's continuing intimacy with Roosevelt and Attorney General Moody made him as informed as he was ardent. If Dolliver could with the Democrats model the bill to Roosevelt's satisfaction and then bring it out of committee as a party measure, he would have thereafter a tactical advantage. In these parts, Aldrich did not try to shape the bill in committee. He could not have persuaded a majority to go his way, but he could and did persuade a majority to ease his way. Seeming to yield, disarming Dolliver, Aldrich permitted the Hepburn Bill to be reported unamended. Then, supported by Democratic votes on which Dolliver had counted, he secured a motion reserving to each committee member the right to propose amendments from the floor. The issue, still unresolved, was now before the whole Senate.

The same Democratic votes sustained Aldrich's next move. Had Dolliver, as he expected, been designated to guide the measure on the floor, he would still have been an asset to the President and the bill might still have been presented as the party's. Almost the senator from Iowa could see the "Hepburn-Dolliver Act" engraved in history. The Democrats, however, de-

siring some credit for regulating railroads, preferred that half
that title belong to them. This preference Aldrich exploited. He
had won the Democrats in the committee to reporting the bill for
amendment from the floor by arranging to name as its floor
leader one of their party, Benjamin Tillman of South Carolina.
With that serpent-tongued agrarian as its guide, the bill could
not be labeled "Republican." For Dolliver this was a staggering
personal blow; for Aldrich, a beguiling triumph; for Roosevelt, an
embarrassing problem in communication. The President and Tillman had long loathed each other. Only recently the senator had
made one of his calculated, insulting attacks on Roosevelt's
character. For years they had not spoken. Now Aldrich had
forced them either to coöperate or to endanger the policy they
both espoused. Whatever their course, furthermore, Aldrich had
moved the bill into a position where he and his collaborators had
an excellent change of neutralizing it by amendment. "Aldrich,"
Roosevelt concluded irritably, had "completely lost both his head
and his temper." The President had lost the first round.

Well before the Hepburn Bill reached the Senate, Aldrich and
his associates had determined on the nature of their attack. Perhaps out of deference to the electorate, they refrained from a
direct assault on the maximum rate clause. Instead, they concentrated on amendments by which they intended to endow the
judiciary, the least mobile of the branches of government, with
the authority to nullify and to delay the rate rulings of the I.C.C.
In behalf of these amendments they debated not the economics
of rate-making or the proprieties of privilege, but the constitutionality of the regulatory process, the orderly system that the
President proposed to create.

Roosevelt had noted with care that the I.C.C. or a substitute
commission "should be made unequivocably administrative." To
an administrative body as opposed to an executive department,
Congress could, he believed, within the meaning of the Constitution on the separation of powers, delegate the authority to fix
maximum rates. This has become a commonplace assumption, the

basis of a proliferation of alphabet agencies, but in 1906 men of disinterested conviction as well as those who were sheer obstructionists questioned the legality of combining in one body the quasi-legislative power of determining rates, even maximum rates, the quasi-judicial authority of deciding upon the validity of rates, and the quasi-executive function of investigation and enforcement. The unsuccessful railroad bill of 1905, attempting to resolve this constitutional difficulty, had included a clause, briefly resuscitated in 1910 by the Mann-Elkins Act, establishing a special court of commerce to review the rate decisions of the I.C.C. The Hepburn Bill as it emerged from the House, however, made no similar provision. Dodging the whole issue of judicial review, it said nothing at all about jurisdiction in cases arising under it.

On the question of judicial review, the proponents and the opponents of Roosevelt's program drew their lines. Contrasted to the large and varied significance of the whole railroad measure, this deployment seems at first almost chicane. Yet since the debates on Hamilton's reports, American legislators had persisted in clothing their differences in constitutional terms. Nor, in the case of the Hepburn Bill, was this lawyers' legacy meaningless. Roosevelt envisioned a new kind of federal executive power to control the complex processes of an industrialized state. He anticipated the methods of the future. His opponents in the Senate, seeking to perpetuate the method or lack of method of the past, relied upon the prevailing dicta of the American courts to prevent the executive from interfering in the day-by-day operations of American business. In government based on law, this was in 1906 still a legal as well as an economic issue. Both sides assiduously spoke the Constitution fair.

The President by no means denied the right of judicial review. He did not believe that any legislation could "prevent . . . an appeal" from a ruling of the I.C.C. "The courts will retain, and should retain, no matter what the Legislature does," he had asserted, "the power to interfere and upset any action that is confiscatory in its nature." Yet Roosevelt also preferred that judicial review should be limited essentially to procedural questions — to a determination, in any mooted case, of whether the commission's method of reaching the decision had been fair to the carrier. His opponents, on the other hand, hoped to emasculate his program by providing explicitly for broad judicial reinterpretation of the facts of each case. This would have given the courts, considered friendly by the railroads, rather than the commission, which the railroads feared, the real authority over rates.

By its reticence on the matter, the House's version of the Hepburn Bill left to the courts themselves the determination of the scope of review. Roosevelt expressed his satisfaction with this evasion. Attorney General Moody, however, advised him that the measure, in order to pass the test of constitutionality, needed an amendment affirming the right of the railroads to have the courts review the commission's decisions. Roosevelt then considered it only desirable but not essential that the bill provide narrow review. As he began negotiations with the leaders of the Senate, he sought not a limitation to procedural review but only an ambiguous declaration, consonant with the evasion in the unamended version, of the right of review.

Inherent in, but in Roosevelt's opinion subordinate to, the problem of the scope of judicial review was the question of the time at which the rate decisions of the I.C.C. should become effective. Roosevelt had asked that they take effect "immediately," a stipulation the Hepburn Bill fulfilled to his satisfaction by making them effective in thirty days. But if the railroads took to court a decision of the commission, the long process of litigation would postpone indefinitely the application of the revised maximum rate. The House had avoided this problem. In the Senate, while the friends of the railroads wanted just such a delay, the advocates of regulation endeavored to construct some amendment that would prevent the use of injunctions to suspend, pending the outcome of litigation, the rulings of the commission. Roosevelt when debate began preferred, but, as on the question of narrow review, did not insist that the use of injunctions be restricted.

Against the President's moderate, almost uncertain, position the prorailroad senators launched an offensive. Philander Chase Knox, who had while Attorney General seemed to endorse Roosevelt's program, refused in a conference with Moody to reach an agreement on an amendment pertaining to judicial review. Moody's draft, supported by the President, protected the constitutionality of the Hepburn Bill without increasing the appellate jurisdiction of the courts. This was not enough for Knox. In conference he stated that he preferred the House's bill to Moody's amendment. To the Senate he proposed in February that the courts pass on the "lawfulness" of the commission's orders — a term Moody considered so vague as to invite continuing litigation on the economic details and constitutional implications of each rate order. Knox's broad definition of review, carrying as it did the prestige of its author, provided in compelling form precisely the objective of Aldrich and his allies. To graft upon the Hepburn Bill Knox's amendment or one just like it, Aldrich had maneuvered the measure out of committee and onto the floor.

Roosevelt, while Aldrich deployed, had not been idle. From the time the Hepburn Bill reached the Senate, even as it lay in committee, the President had begun to confer with his Republican associates about amendments. Like Aldrich, he had able collaborators. Most helpful of these were William B. Allison of Iowa and John C. Spooner of Wisconsin who, in other years, had with Aldrich and the now deceased O. H. Platt composed the Senate's inner council of control. Allison, of that Four the most sensitive to the tolerances of public opinion and the most skillful negotiator, "rendered," Roosevelt later recalled, "unwearied and invaluable service in the actual, and indispensable, working out of legislative business." Spooner, scarcely less gifted, had a large personal stake in the satisfactory resolution of the problem of regulation, for his home bastion rattled before the guerrillas of the insurgent La Follette. Allison and Spooner brought with them a loyal corps of lesser Western Republican veterans for whom freight rates had assumed pressing political importance. The President could also rely upon, though he would not confide in, the intense Republican left. Could these men clearly demonstrate their strength, others in the party would reluctantly go their way. Finally, there were the Bryan Democrats, Tillman, Bailey of Texas, and a few more cautious in thought and less erratic in deportment who would probably damn Roosevelt's bill but give it their votes.

So positioned, Roosevelt planned at first to carry the bill by sponsoring amendments which would attract the Republican center without alienating the bipartisan left. Throughout February and much of March, while the bill lay in committee, he sought only to perpetuate explicitly the ambiguities implicit in the House's version. The plan seemed feasible so long as the committee might fashion a party measure. But Aldrich's coup, preventing this, also permitted the senator to vitiate Roosevelt's influence with the uncertain. Naturally like Aldrich disposed to trust the judiciary to brake change, the Republican center, relieved of party discipline, now looked more favorably on broad review. Tillman as floor leader for the bill was scarcely fit by temperament or inclination to dissuade them. The President, consequently, had to adjust his strategy to Aldrich's *démarche*.

Roosevelt acted at once. As his personal, unofficial representative in the Senate he selected Allison, who could reach and convince a larger number of Republicans than could have any other possible agent. He arranged also to communicate with Tillman through ex-Senator William E. Chandler, a mutual friend and advocate of regulation. By this clumsy device, with Tillman's help and through Allison's negotiations, Roosevelt then set out to construct a new coalition. "Inasmuch as the Republican leaders have tried to betray me . . . ," he explained, "I am now trying to see if I cannot get . . . [the bill] through in the form I want by the aid of some fifteen or twenty Republicans added to most of the Democrats." For this purpose, involving as it did both the enthusiasm of Tillman and the loyalty of Allison, Roosevelt had to move cautiously but clearly to the left of his original position.

Largely to Allison fell the difficult task of seeking a formula which would solve the problems of judicial review and the use of injunctions to the satisfaction of the divers partners to the potential coalition. Aldrich, if not surprised, must have been a little hurt to find his friend working the other side of the aisle. The work was tedious. Senator after senator contributed to the dozens of amendments under consideration. Three of these sufficiently reveal the nature of Allison's predicament. That of Senator Long of Kansas, the well-advertised product of a White House conference held just at the time Roosevelt decided to rely upon a coalition, prevented, according to the consensus of the Senate, judicial reconsideration of the facts of a case. In endorsing it, the President, no longer equivocal, won the favor of the coalition's Republicans and populist Democrats. Yet this was not enough. Senator Bailey of Texas, Tillman's closest associate, and other persistent Jeffersonians opposed the amendment, as Aldrich expected they would, because it seemed to them an unwarranted extension of executive power. Both Tillman and Bailey, moreover, considered the injunction issue more important than judicial review. The Texan had introduced an amendment, endorsed by most Democrats, which deprived the courts of authority to issue temporary writs suspending rate orders. Although this proposal effectively prevented delay in the application of rate rulings, it seemed to Roosevelt and his harassed lieutenants to be clearly unconstitutional. As negotiations proceeded, the President feared that Aldrich might adopt Bailey's plan or any of several like it in order with Democratic support to write a law that the courts would promptly nullify. Roosevelt and Allison therefore sponsored as an alternative an amendment drafted by Spooner. It provided that whenever a court suspended a rate order the amount in dispute between the carrier and the commission should be placed in escrow pending the outcome of litigation. Spooner's plan at once prevented confiscation of railroad property without due process of law, protected the shippers, and eliminated any advantage for the railroad in seeking litigation simply to cause delay.

Had Roosevelt and Allison been dealing only with resilient men, such ingenuity as Spooner's might, in time, have permitted them to devise a winning compromise. Bailey, for one, began to trim toward Allison. But a few Republicans and Tillman Democrats remained so adamantly for narrow review, many other Democrats so firmly for broad review, that Spooner's promising solution for injunctions never commanded the serious attention of either extreme. Before Allison had a chance to homogenize these stubborn parts, Aldrich precipitated crisis. He, too, had been active across the aisle. On April 18, as he predicted, the Democratic caucus refused to follow Tillman and Bailey. Roosevelt's attempt at coalition had failed.

Aldrich, the second round his, doubtless hoped that Roosevelt would either capitulate or, as he had a few weeks earlier, move further left. The President could have consolidated a noisy defense by throwing in his lot with the La Follette Republicans and Tillman Democrats. He could with them have swelled the rising voices of protest. He might, by such a move, have earned a popularity beyond even that already his. But he would have lost his bill. Seeing this as clearly as did Aldrich, Roosevelt had already prepared once more to redeploy.

Six days earlier, sensing defeat, the President had begun to hedge. If he could not win with Tillman, he might still win on his own original terms without the Democrats. "I am not at all sure," he then wrote Allison, "but that the easy way will be to come right back to the bill as it passed the House, and with very few unimportant amendments to pass it as it stands." On April 22 Roosevelt told Knox, again his confidant, that this opinion was "evidently gaining ground." Indeed it was, for Nelson Aldrich turned toward Roosevelt after the Democrats turned away. The leaders of the President's Republican opposition by early May ceased to insist on an explicit statement for broad review. Perhaps Aldrich became impatient with the continuing delay in the work of the Senate brought about by the everlasting debate on regulation. Perhaps he decided that Republican solidarity was more important than Roosevelt's purpose was dangerous. Probably, however, he saw that he had miscalculated. When Roosevelt, refusing to list with the left, reverted doggedly to the ambiguous center where he had first stood, he impelled Tillman, La Follette, and their likes, his erstwhile allies, into embittered opposition. Their protestations, couched in their inevitable vocabulary of revolt, attested to the safe reasonableness Roosevelt had ever claimed as his own. The uncertain minds of the wavering Republican center might now hear Allison out — might now, as Allison and Spooner had, see in Roosevelt safety. By some new alignment, like that he had hoped Dolliver would muster, the President with time in *Thermidor* might triumph. At least, so Aldrich may have reasoned. In any case he retreated.

He may also have drafted the amendment which, introduced by Allison, won a majority vote and thereby secured the enactment of the Hepburn Bill. Whether or not Aldrich drafted it, Allison's amendment, leaving the bill in effect as the House had written it, gave Roosevelt what he had started out to get. The authorship of the amendment, like the working of Aldrich's mind, remains obscure. Whoever wrote it, Allison guided it. His activities in the two weeks following the Democratic caucus may be accurately surmised. Leaving no records, the "unwearied and invaluable" senator from Iowa, camped in the cloakroom where he excelled, had fashioned for the President a compromise that satisfied enough Republicans to save the bill.

The Allison amendment covered both judicial review and the use of injunctions. With purposeful obscurity, it granted jurisdiction in cases arising under the Hepburn Act to the circuit courts but left the definition of the scope of review to the courts. In a flood of oratory over the meaning of the amendment, each senator interpreted it to suit himself and his constituents. Both sides claimed victory. Insofar as the amendment was described as a victory for either narrow or broad review, the claims were non-sense. The question of review remained in May as unsettled as it had been in February. Roosevelt had then asked for no more. Ultimately the Supreme Court, which he trusted so little, in the first decision involving rate rulings made his preference law by refusing to review the facts of the case.

The Allison amendment did affirmatively settle the matter of injunctions by empowering the courts to "enjoin, set aside, annul, or suspend any order" of the I.C.C. It also prescribed that appeals from the orders of the I.C.C. were to go directly to the Supreme Court with the calendar priorities of antitrust cases. The amendment did not, however, specify the grounds for suspension or establish an escrow scheme. There remained, consequently, the possibility of considerable delay before rate rulings took effect. Roosevelt had constantly expressed his preference for an arrangement less favorable to the railroads, but he had also continually indicated that he would accept a solution like that of the Allison amendment. On this matter Tillman and Bailey, but neither Aldrich nor Roosevelt, had been defeated.

Roosevelt was "entirely satisfied" with the Allison amendment, he pointed out, because he was "entirely satisfied with the Hepburn bill." The amendment, he informed a less satisfied representative of midwestern shippers, was "only declaratory of what the Hepburn bill must mean, supposing it to be constitutional . . . I should be glad to get certain [other] amendments . . . ; but they are not vital, and even without them the Hepburn bill with the Allison amendment contains practically exactly what I have both originally and always since asked for."

Characteristically, Roosevelt overstated his case. "Always since" did not apply, for in his maneuvers of late March and April, although only at that time, the President had asked for more. Tillman and Bailey, who had joined him then, with rankling disappointment attacked him for returning to what he had originally requested. Their attacks, often repeated by their friends, have persuaded two generations that Roosevelt, irresolute and insincere, deserting his friends, yielding to Aldrich, lost the battle for regulation. Surely his detractors felt this, but they erred. Roosevelt had made overtures to Tillman and Bailey only for tactical reasons. He had, temporarily and for parliamentary support, enlarged his earlier demands. When this did not produce sufficient support, he reverted for tactical reasons to his first position. In so doing he deserted his temporary allies, but he did not compromise his policy. Tillman and Bailey, proud veterans of the Senate, perhaps resented most the knowledge that they had been used. Doubtless their pain gave Aldrich, who had made Roosevelt woo them and leave them, some amused satisfaction.

His objective attained, Roosevelt exulted. "No given measure and no given set of measures," he believed, "will work a perfect cure for any serious evil; and the insistence upon having only the perfect cure often results in securing no betterment whatever." The Hepburn Act was not perfect. But, Roosevelt maintained, it represented "the longest step ever yet taken in the direction of solving the railway rate problem." This was a fair assessment. With his clear perception of political situations, Roosevelt had set the highest practicable goal. By his mastery of political devices, in contest with another master, he had reached it. The Senate, in the end, supplied the federal executive with authority beyond any antecedent definition to mitigate the maladjustments of a growing industrial society.

The Hepburn Act endowed the Interstate Commerce Commission with power commensurate with its task. By informed, expert decisions, it could at last alter the artificial configurations of a market that had long since ceased, in the classic sense, to be free. The courts inexpertly had judged transportation by criteria which, however precious in jurisprudence, bore little relation to the economics of the process. Released from the inhibition of judicial reinterpretations (the bond that Aldrich had sought to supply), endowed with weapons the carriers respected, the I.C.C. began to develop after 1906 the techniques of effective supervision. The need for further change of course remained. But the Hepburn Act provided the precedent, accepted by the courts and enlarged by later Congresses, by which federal regulatory agencies have promoted the national welfare. Now vastly ramified, government by administrative commission remains, though somewhat shabby, a useful part of American political arrangements.

For a troubled people in a complex time perhaps only the executive could have become steward. Aldrich, in that case, fought history and Roosevelt only accelerated what no man could have prevented. But Roosevelt's reputation rests securely even in acceleration, for the inevitable sometimes takes too long, and he knew just what he did. His efforts in behalf of the Hepburn Act — a measure meaningful but moderate — demonstrated his skilled concern for creating the instruments he thought the nation needed. For an orderly administrative system, for the right of efficient federal controls, for the positive government of an industrial society, he mobilized in a crucial first skirmish the full powers of his office. And he won.

Only continuous, disinterested administrative action, Roosevelt believed, not intermittent lawsuits or intermittent legislation, not the dicta of the bench or the dicta of partisan and sectional politics, could properly direct the development of American industrial society. This conviction related intimately to his feelings about power and its uses. These in their general implications — both domestic and international — must now be elaborated and explored.

Chapter VII

USES OF POWER

"The word happiness," Lionel Trilling has proposed, "stands at the very center" of liberal thought.* It is a word which Theodore Roosevelt used rarely when speaking of himself and almost never when referring to other people. This was not an accident. Roosevelt concerned himself not with happiness but with hard work, duty, power, order. These conditions he valued not as prerequisites for some ultimate happiness but as ends in themselves. All interrelated, they blanketed myriad specifics. Hard work involved, among other things, an identity with task, whether the mining of coal or the writing of history; it was a part of duty and a preliminary of order. Duty demanded alike service to the nation, productive labor, and devoted attention to family. It demanded also physical and intellectual courage, honesty, and constancy. These qualities can produce frightening obstacles to personal happiness. There is a story that Roosevelt, more than two years after the death of his first wife, while contemplating his second marriage, for three days paced in a small guest room of a friend's home, pounding one fist into the other palm, expostulating the while to himself: "I have no constancy. I have no constancy." Not even in love was Roosevelt a liberal.

Roosevelt's politics, certainly, pertained not at all to happiness. There was none of Bentham, none of Mill in his public pronouncements or his private letters. Like those more reflective men, Roosevelt had a good deal of difficulty in defining his beliefs, but manifestly he believed in power and in order. With

* Lionel Trilling, *The Liberal Imagination* (New York, 1950), p. xii.

power he sought to impose order; only with order, he contended, could there be morality.

Because after his fortieth year Roosevelt experienced no major change of thought, all this, inherent in his early thinking, contained the substance of his behavior as President. But during his Presidency he came better to understand himself, and with this new understanding he formalized, candidly and rather consistently, the principles that underlay his purpose. Distinct long before Herbert Croly wrote his *Promise of American Life,* these principles in 1912 provided Roosevelt with a rationalization, indeed with some motivation, for his devastating departure from the Republican party. Consequently they merit analysis not only in themselves but also as a measure of the conduct of the man.

Roosevelt began with power. Attaining it, he appreciated the chase and the reward. "There inheres in the Presidency," he observed, "more power than in any other office in any great republic or constitutional monarchy of modern times . . ." "I believe," he added, "in a strong executive; I believe in power . . ." This conclusion Roosevelt fortified with Hegelian conviction. The animal energy of that "bore as big as a buffalo" that so distressed Henry Adams provided the very force on which Roosevelt unerringly relied. Heroes, he knew, were not made by epigrams. His audiences of "townspeople, . . . of rough-coated, hard-headed, gaunt, sinewy farmers . . . their wives and daughters and . . . children . . . ," he sensed, "for all the superficial differences between us, down at bottom" had "the same ideals . . ." "I am always sure of reaching them," he confided to John Hay, "in speeches which many of my Harvard friends would think not only homely, but commonplace." "The people who believed in me and trusted me and followed me . . . ," Roosevelt asserted, felt that "I was the man of all others whom they wished to see President." Such confidence sustained heroic moods.

Every executive officer, in particular the President, Roosevelt maintained, "was a steward of the people bound actively and affirmatively to do all he could for the people . . ." He held therefore that, unless specifically forbidden by the Constitution or by law, the President had "to do anything that the needs of the nation demanded . . ." "Under this interpretation of executive power," he recalled, "I did and caused to be done many things not previously done . . . I did not usurp power, but I did greatly broaden the use of executive power." To this interpretation, Roosevelt confessed, his temperament compelled him. So, of course, did his profession; elected or appointed, the bureaucrat would exalt his valleys. Realizing this, the second Charles Francis Adams feared a regulatory bureaucracy as much as he despised the competitive confusion it was intended to stabilize. Not so Roosevelt. He broadened power precisely for the purpose of establishing order.

Throughout his life, Roosevelt displayed a morbid fear of social violence which, he seemed to feel, lay ominously on the margin of normal political life. He convinced himself that William Jennings Bryan, Eugene V. Debs, the Socialist leader, and Big Bill Haywood of the Industrial Workers of the World had inherited the mission of Marat and Robespierre. This was not just campaign hyperbole. In season and out, with wearing repetition he discovered the Jacobin in each dissenter of his time. To their evil he apposed a twin, the evil of those "malefactors of great wealth" who on lower Broadway held their court of Louis XVI. Unleashed, the energies of these extremes could in conflict wreck society. They had therefore to be curtailed.

To modulate the threatening conflict Roosevelt in part relied upon that indefinite composite which he called national character. He meant by this not only personal morality but also the conglutinations that history prepared, the accepted traditions of political and social behavior by which people imposed order on themselves. Yet these traditions, he recognized, depended heavily upon material conditions which in the twentieth century were changing rapidly. The change Roosevelt welcomed; he foresaw more strength than danger in the new industrialism. But it demanded, he realized, concomitant political changes whose contours tradition could not draw.

If self-imposed order was in his time no longer to be anticipated, it had to be provided from above. This called for strong, disinterested government equipped to define, particularly for a powerful executive prepared to enforce, the revised rules under which the America of immense corporations, of enormous cities, of large associations of labor and farmers could in orderly manner resolve its conflicts. Definition and enforcement were needed at once, for within the lifetime of Roosevelt's older contemporaries social relations had changed "far more rapidly than in the preceding two centuries." The ensuing weaknesses in traditional political behavior strained the fabric of personal morality. In the United States of 1908, the President remarked in his perceptive last annual message to Congress, "the chief breakdown is in dealing with the new relations that arise from the mutualism, the interdependence of our time. Every new social relation begets a new type of wrong-doing — of sin, to use an old-fashioned word — and many years always elapse before society is able to turn this sin into crime which can be effectively punished at law."

Through mutualism itself Roosevelt hoped to stabilize social arrangements. His recommendations were designed first to create a political environment favorable to social and economic combinations which, he believed, the nation needed, and second, ordinarily through responsible administrative agencies, to prescribe the rules for the operation of those combinations. American industry afforded a salubrious example of "the far-reaching, beneficent work" which combination had already accomplished. In steel alone a Spencerian progression from the simple heterogeneous to the complex homogeneous suggested the almost limitless possibilities of power and productivity. Such a progression, Roosevelt believed, neither should nor could be arrested. But it had to be disciplined. Combinations in industry, susceptible as they were to the temptations of unbridled power, had to be made responsible through government to the whole people. They had, furthermore, to be balanced by other, also responsible combinations, voluntarily formed to promote the efficiency of less well organized parts of society. "This is an era," Roosevelt preached, "of federation and combination . . ."

"A simple and poor society," he later postulated, "can exist as a democracy on a basis of sheer individualism. But a rich and complex industrial society cannot so exist; for some individuals, and especially those artificial individuals called corporations, become so very big that the ordinary individual . . . cannot deal with them on terms of equality. It therefore becomes necessary for these ordinary individuals to combine in their turn, first in order to act in their collective capacity through that biggest of all combinations called the government, and second, to act, also in their own self-defense, through private combinations, such as farmers' associations and trade-unions."

Attempting as he did to apply this doctrine to agriculture, labor and industry, Roosevelt envisioned an equilibrium of consolidated interests over which government would preside. To the farmer his purpose appealed least. Roosevelt was, after all, primarily an eastern, urban man. He had never fully understood the dreadful anxieties that underlay the agrarian movements of the 1890s or the deficiencies in national banking and credit arrangements that aggravated farm finance. He developed his program, furthermore, at a time when agricultural prosperity tended to obscure even for farmers the continuing weaknesses of their situation. Nevertheless, much of his advice was sound.

"Farmers must learn," Roosevelt proposed, "the vital need of co-operation with one another. Next to this comes co-operation with the government, and the government can best give its aid through associations of farmers rather than through the individual farmer . . . It is greatly to be wished . . . that associations of farmers could be organized, primarily for business purposes, but also with social ends in view . . . The people of our farming regions must be able to combine among themselves, as the most efficient means of protecting their industry from the highly organized interests which now surround them on every side. A vast field is open for work by co-operative associations of farmers in dealing with the relation of the farm to transportation and to the distribution and manufacture of raw materials. It is only through such combination that American farmers can develop to the full their economic and social power."

Through the Department of Agriculture, within the restrictive limits of its budget and authority, Roosevelt promoted farm co-operatives. To the recommendations of farm associations about changes in national transportation policy he gave a sympathetic hearing. "To ascertain what are the general, economic, social, educational, and sanitary conditions of the open country, and what, if anything, the farmers themselves can do to help themselves, and how the Government can help them," he appointed in 1908 the Country Life Commission. The report of this commission, although ignored by a Congress which refused even to appropriate funds for its printing, was a landmark in national thinking about the melioration of almost every aspect of rural life. To it, as to Roosevelt's own counsel, federal administrations later profitably returned.

Roosevelt intended that farm life should become increasingly institutionalized. While he urged this, he expected the farmers voluntarily to form their own organizations. Still the most individualistic-minded of Americans, they proceeded slowly. He could not command them, as he advised them, to exploit more fully the bicycle and the telephone; he could not force them to emulate the marketing coöperatives of Denmark. Consequently the immediate results of his advice were negligible. When he acted himself, however, instead of simply urging them to act, he accomplished more. His employment of the strength of the government, especially of his office, imposed upon the country a conservation policy from which the farmers, however much they disliked it at the time, ultimately benefited.

Roosevelt sponsored conservation not so much to preserve a

domain for agriculture as to preserve and enhance the strength of the whole nation. He was inspired not by farmers and ranchers but by intellectuals and interested commercial groups. Nevertheless, in effect his policy organized an essential element of prosperous rural existence. This it did directly through the irrigation act which compelled its beneficiaries to mutualism. Indirectly, Roosevelt's public power policy, resisting uncontrolled exploitation of water power sites, began to reserve control of power for the federal government. Through government agencies, interests of agriculture could be consolidated and advanced. By "planned and orderly development" — "essential to the best use of every natural resource" — these agencies could define and attain objectives which farmers' organizations, even if they had had the perspicacity to define, lacked the authority to attain. The varied purposes of his power policy, the need to restrain the haphazard and selfish methods of private direction, and the inadequacies of voluntary associations alike persuaded the President that for orderly development order had to be established from above.

Much more favorably than did the farmers, American labor responded to Roosevelt's doctrine of federation and combination. Agrarian spokesmen at the turn of the century, still antimonopolists in their orientation, proposed to solve the trust problem by disintegrating industrial combinations. The representatives of organized labor, on the contrary, intended to live with big business by bargaining with it. The general secretary of the United Garment Workers, the head of the United Mine Workers, and the president of the American Federation of Labor, among others, accepting the consolidation of industry as inevitable and salutary, sought to lead labor to comparable consolidations and to persuade government to protect the processes of combination and negotiation. Roosevelt spoke, therefore, to a receptive audience when he maintained that labor should reap "the benefits of organization," that wageworkers had "an entire right to organize" and "a legal right . . . to refuse to work in company with men who decline to join their organizations."

Repeatedly Roosevelt acted upon this principle. He drew upon the advice of the leaders of the railroad brotherhoods and the American Federation of Labor in fashioning his recommendations to Congress for legislation to govern the hours and working conditions of women and children, to extend the eight-hour day, to provide for comprehensive employers' liability, and to improve railroad safety precautions.* During the most celebrated strike of his term in office, his intercession defended the right of the anthracite miners to bargain collectively. Continually he endeavored to restrict the use of injunctions, the most formidable weapon against labor. The court's order prohibiting boycotting in the Buck's Case he criticized severely; he ordered the Justice Department to assist an iron molders' local whose strike had been enjoined. There must, Roosevelt insisted, "be no . . . abuse of the injunctive power as is implied in forbidding laboring men to strive for their own betterment in peaceful and lawful ways; nor must the injunction be used merely to aid some big corporation . . . a preliminary injunction in a labor case, if granted without adequate proof . . . may often settle the dispute . . . and therefore if improperly granted may do irreparable wrong . . . I earnestly commend . . . that some way may be devised which will limit the abuse of injunctions and protect those rights which from time to time it unwarrantably invades."

---

* Roosevelt also agreed with Gompers and other craft union leaders who argued that mass immigration from the Orient and from southern and eastern Europe impaired labor's ability to organize. These immigrants — the labor unionizers held — willing to work for low wages, unfamiliar with American ways, were difficult if not impossible to organize. To protect American labor they therefore advocated the restriction of immigration, first of Asiatics, later also of Europeans. Roosevelt's attitudes toward immigration restriction were at most times close to those of labor leaders, not so much because they influenced him as because he shared their prejudices, as did so many Americans. Although he praised some unions for their work in Americanization, he generally failed to understand that the craft unions could not organize immigrant labor largely because they would not try.

Encouraged to bargain, allowed to strike, the union was to consolidate the interests of labor. This had value for Roosevelt insofar as it promoted efficiency and order. But some unions, like the syndicalist Industrial Workers of the World, cultivated violence; some labor leaders, like the socialist Debs, defending these unions, seemed to Roosevelt to court revolution. To handle such cases, he believed it "wrong altogether to prohibit the use of injunctions," for "there must be no hesitation in dealing with disorder."

The measure of order, difficult at best, Roosevelt would not leave to the judiciary. During and immediately after his tenure, the courts granted injunctions indiscriminately and nullified much of the labor legislation he considered necessary and just. Underwriting as they did the status quo, they prevented the very changes upon which, he felt, a new social equilibrium depended. It was judicial interpretation of labor law that motivated Roosevelt finally to propose the recall of judicial decisions, a system which referred the interpretation of the needs of society to a momentary majority of the people. Conversely, Roosevelt was impatient with the legal impediments to silencing a Debs or a Haywood. Order for him was order. If a man incited violence, if he only endeavored to incite violence, indeed if he merely defended the prerogative of another man to incite violence, Roosevelt yearned at once to stamp him underfoot.

In dealing with radical newspapers and with the syndicalist Western Federation of Miners, Roosevelt, assuming the prerogatives of a steward of the people, decreed from his high office dicta of order with which many peaceable men could not conscientiously agree. By the same standard, while President he initiated a criminal libel suit — a suit presuming an offense against the United States — against a publisher who had criticized him, and he kept in prison without legal sanction a petty criminal who had violated not a law but his concept of the right. Such lawless uses of power, however meritorious or moral their intent, undermined the traditional principles of restraint upon which American order had been built. This created a danger that labor leaders recognized. They had too often been the victims of arbitrary power — ordinarily industrial rather than political — to trust completely any man who proposed himself to decide when their contests were safe and when they were not.

Labor had other reservations about Roosevelt. Just short of the full meaning of his preachments he stopped. On the issue of injunctions, he retreated in 1908 when the Republican National Convention did. Bryan, Brandeis and for a while Woodrow Wilson made no such forced marches. Furthermore, Roosevelt's doctrine of consolidation did not quite possess him. He would consolidate for order and also to establish the prescriptions for morality. But in the end he measured morality by the individual. "The chief factor in the success of each man — ," he asserted, "wageworker, farmer, and capitalist alike — must ever be the sum total of his own individual qualities and abilities. Second only to this comes the power of acting in combination or association with others." He judged on this basis that the "legal right" of wageworkers "to refuse to work in company with men who decline to join their organizations" might or might not, "according to circumstances," be a "moral right." There fell the union shop. Roosevelt reserved to himself definition of the moral right. He sustained the open shop in the Government Printing Office because he did not consider the circumstances a proper legal or moral basis for unionization. Where could he or his successor be expected next to draw the line?

The farmer could at once agree with Roosevelt about the primacy of individual qualities. The industrialist, protected by the legal fiction that a corporation — whatever its size — was an individual, could accept this dictum. Not so the labor leader. If the union did not contain every interested individual, its position relative to management suffered, and its victories benefited neutral noncontributors. This for labor leaders was a question not of morality but of money and of power. The President's ambivalence confused their issue.

In Roosevelt's program the farm community found discomforting unfamiliarity; about it union labor entertained anxious doubts. Businessmen were more enthusiastic, for from industry and transportation Roosevelt took his model. With accelerating tempo for two generations men of business had made consolidation their instrument not only of profits but also, more significantly, of order. Abandoning the insecurity and debilitation of competition, the enterprising in rails, steel, oil, copper, tobacco, sugar, salt — the list seems endless — had, after strife, in each industry organized stable structures. Their own achievement they admired. It was, they testified at symposiums on trusts, to congressional committees, in essays, memoirs and commencement addresses, the necessary and efficient way of business life, perhaps the only way of any life. With few exceptions they wished to have their institutions left alone. Here only did Roosevelt disagree. Because the consolidations were.capable of doing much that was bad as well as much that was good, they had to be supervised. But they were not to be destroyed. "In curbing and regulating the combinations of capital which are . . . injurious . . . ," he instructed Congress in his second annual message, "we must be careful not to stop the great enterprises which have legitimately reduced the cost of production, not to abandon the place which our country has won in the leadership of the international industrial world . . ."

Again and again during his Presidency Roosevelt made the distinction between size and behavior that characterized his speeches of 1912 on the regulation of industry. For the orderly system of control in which he believed he first shaped his railroad policy. In developing that policy, he announced his preference for supervised pooling as an efficient regulatory device. Enlarging his thesis, he asserted late in 1911 that "nothing of importance is gained by breaking up a huge inter-State and international industrial organization *which has not offended otherwise than by its size* . . . Those who would seek to restore the days of unlimited and uncontrolled competition . . . are attempting not only the impossible, but what, if possible, would be undesirable." "Business cannot be successfully conducted," he wrote in the same article, "in accordance with the practices and theories of sixty years ago unless we abolish steam, electricity, big cities, and, in short, not only all modern business and modern industrial conditions, but all the modern conditions of our civilization." This statement recognized associationalism as being as much a part of modern life as were the physical conditions that compelled it. Roosevelt also realized that, just as government could best supply a "planned and orderly development" of natural resources, so was oligopoly distinguished by its ability to provide experts to plan and to allocate from profits adequate resources to implement their plans — by its ability, therefore, to keep order without stultification.

But business had "to be controlled in the interest of the general public" and this could be accomplished in only one way — "by giving adequate power of control to the one sovereignty capable of exercising such power — the National Government." As an initial means for this control Roosevelt led Congress to establish the Bureau of Corporations. In his long struggle for the Hepburn Act he went considerably further. He next concluded and soon specifically proposed that "what is needed is the creation of a Federal administrative body with full power to do for ordinary inter-State industrial business carried on on a large scale what the Inter-State Commerce Commission now does for inter-State transportation business."

After leaving the Presidency, in the columns of *The Outlook* Roosevelt elaborated his plan. He would "regulate big corporations in thoroughgoing and effective fashion, so as to help legitimate business as an incident to thoroughly and completely safeguarding the interests of the people as a whole." The antitrust law, designed and interpreted "to restore business to the competitive conditions of the middle of the last century," could not "meet the whole situation." Size did indeed "make a corporation fraught with potential menace to the community," but the community could "exercise through its administrative . . . officers a strict supervision . . . to see that it does not go wrong," "to insure . . . business skill being exercised in the interest of the public . . ."

Criticizing the suit initiated by the Taft Administration against the United States Steel Corporation, and deploring the vagueness of the Supreme Court's "rule of reason" in the Standard Oil and tobacco cases, Roosevelt explained how "continuous administrative action" might operate. The commission to regulate corporations was to have the power to regulate the issue of securities, thereby to prevent overcapitalization; to compel publicity of accounts, thereby to reveal the detailed techniques of business procedures; and to investigate any business activity. If investigation disclosed the existence of monopoly — of a consolidation that could control the prices and productivity of an industry — the commission was to have two alternatives. If unethical practices had produced monopoly — Roosevelt cited the oil and tobacco industries as examples of this — the monopoly should be dissolved under the Sherman Act. If, however, the monopoly resulted from natural growth — Roosevelt had in mind the United States Steel Corporation and the International Harvester Company — the commission was to control it by setting maximum prices for its products, just as the I.C.C. set maximum freight rates. This was not all. Believing that administrative control should "indirectly or directly extend to . . . all questions connected with . . . [the] treatment of . . . employees," he proposed that the commission should have authority over hours, wages, and other conditions of labor.

Within each industry, then, consolidation was to establish order; acting in the public interest, the federal executive was to insure equity in this order. This fitted the grand scheme. It also offered to farm and labor groups, through the presumed disinterestedness of government, a countervailing force against the most advanced and, at that time, least controlled social group. By consolidation and administration Roosevelt would punish sin and achieve stability. To discipline consolidation, to make possible administration, his first requisite was power. The cycle was complete.

The question remains of how well this arrangement could be expected to function. Even a sampling of evidence suggests that it raised problems as large as those it presumed to solve. There was, for one, the problem of the natural growth of industrial combinations. Roosevelt considered it, in general terms, desirable. He believed, clearly, that an administrative agency could better judge what was natural growth than could the courts. Furthermore, as his relations with his Attorneys General and his directions to the chairman of the Interstate Commerce Commission indicate, he had considerable confidence in his own capacity to make administrative decisions pertinent to transportation and industry. How then explain the suit against the Northern Securities Company? The defendants in that case had by forming a holding company combined into a potentially efficient regional system the basic units of railway transportation in the Northwest. Railways had for decades been consolidating, naturally enough in the logic of railroad economics. The Northern Securities combination restored financial order among the rivals it merged and seemed capable of becoming a useful part of an orderly, integrated transportation network. Yet in 1902 Roosevelt proceeded against it. One suspects that he would have done so even if the I.C.C. at that time had had the authority to set maximum rates.

Two major considerations apparently motivated Roosevelt. First, the farmers of the Northwest and their local political representatives wanted the holding company dissolved. It was good politics for Roosevelt to attack it. Second, as Roosevelt recalled in his autobiography, "the absolutely vital question" of "whether the government had power to control [corporations] . . . at all . . . had not yet been decided . . . A decision of the Supreme Court [in the E. C. Knight case] had, with seeming definiteness, settled that the National Government had not the power." "This decision," Roosevelt continued, alluding to his prosecution of the Northern Securities Company, "I caused to be annulled . . ." He attacked to establish the government's power, for the while his power; he selected a corporation indisputably engaged in interstate commerce; he deliberately chose to charge a hill made vulnerable by popular opinion. Particularly when used by a man who has and loves power, such criteria may become terrifying.

This possibility Roosevelt intended partially to avoid by his reliance upon experts. Presumably the specialists who were to staff a regulatory commission would be restrained by the data they commanded. Unhappily this need not be the case. Emanating in large degree from the organizations to be controlled, the data explored by administrative commissions can often capture them. In such a pass, regulation may approach consent, and stability become stultification. Nor do experts, any more than other men, live by data alone. Besides common colds and ulcers, they develop loyalties and habits. In government, as in business or in education, administrators become to some extent the victims of their institutions. For many of them, lines of authority and procedure come to have an attraction of their own, an attraction that frequently induces a soporific insistence on inert routine, a fatal disinclination to innovation, sometimes to formalized action beyond the shuffling of bureaucratic dust.

Furthermore, even meaningful, objective data and personal energy and imagination do not necessarily make regulation by administration what Roosevelt thought it might be. He seemed to presume that politics would stop at the commission's water line. In a sense this is true. Railroads petitioning the I.C.C. may in that process be at once all Federalists, all Republicans. But in another sense it is not true. The conflicting interests whose reconciliation politics must effect continue to conflict before the tribunals of administration. In a contest behind closed doors among spokesmen of management, labor and government, the adroit politician will ordinarily prevail.

The possibility remains that the problems of competition, consolidation and control can be resolved more equitably — though perhaps with more waste — in the open environments provided by the legislative or the adversary process. If it is hard to find good congressmen and judges, so is it hard to find good commissioners. And whatever the deficiencies of parliaments and courts, they concern themselves with concrete rules of conduct, written for all to see, by which behavior can be measured. These rules pertain, moreover, not only to citizens and corporations, but also to their public servants.

The conclusion imperiously suggests itself that Roosevelt did not want to be controlled, that he did not want to be inhibited by a body of law, whether or not it was properly interpreted, nor delayed by the impedance of legislatures. He proposed to govern. Basically this was also the desire of the leaders of American industry and finance. Relentless agents of consolidation, they imposed and administered orders of their own. Many of them were willing in the interest of industrial peace to go a long way in condoning combinations formed by union labor. With the leaders of these newer orders they were then prepared, man to man, to bargain. Some of them foresaw that in the society they molded, big government might have to provide balance. Most of them, however, as was the case with Morgan when Roosevelt moved against the Northern Securities Company, thought that they could bargain, man to man, with government. Here they miscalculated. Their rule began to fade when Roosevelt began to make of government a superior rather than a negotiating power.

Yet intellectually and emotionally he was always more one of them than was he an agrarian reformer or a partner of little business and of labor — a Bryan or a La Follette or a Brandeis. Perhaps with a sense of this affinity to men of business, Roosevelt called himself a conservative; and with reference to his difference — to his insistence that the governing was the government's — he added that a true conservative was a progressive. This was the position also of George W. Perkins, who for a time personified articulate finance; of Frank Munsey, consolidator of journalism, like Perkins a Bull Mooser; of Herbert Croly, who promised to American life little that Roosevelt had not already offered; of Brooks Adams, who would have arrested the disintegration of a democracy he never understood by consolidation, conservation, and administration — the very trinity of Roosevelt. To champion consolidation as a means to order, to believe in administration and to practice it well, this was the creed of a business elite in the early century and of that conservative intelligentsia they helped to inspire.

It rested upon a feeling about power that J. Pierpont Morgan, prodded by a congressional committee, disclosed, a feeling to which Roosevelt thoroughly subscribed. Morgan saw nothing wrong about the scope of his power, for he maintained that his morality controlled it. He also arranged that the specialists in his house helped exercise it. Roosevelt made a like claim and like arrangements. Yet Morgan was neither virtuous nor successful in his ventures with the New Haven railroad, and Roosevelt was just as vulnerable to failures of the soul and errors of the flesh. In a nation democratic by intent, Morgan's responsibility to a limited number of investors made his power less acceptable than did Roosevelt's responsibility to the whole electorate, but if their power was relatively responsible, it was in both cases absolutely corruptible.

To his great credit and doubtless greater pain, Roosevelt, understanding this, surrendered his power. Explaining his decision not to be a candidate in 1908, Roosevelt wrote: "I don't think that any harm comes from the concentration of power in one man's hands, provided the holder does not keep it for more than a certain, definite time, and then returns to the people from whom he sprang." This decision was a large achievement of restraint. Roosevelt could certainly have had the Republican nomination and would probably have won the election. The temptations to continue were enormous. Nevertheless he declined. This strength of character supported strongly the claims he made to the use of power; yet it was not enough.

Suppose only that Roosevelt was human and fallible — he need not have been paranoid or depraved, fallibility is here enough — and he claimed too much. Four years or eight years or twelve years, the number of terms is unimportant, may be in the history of this nation a brief and placid time or a tempestuous eternity. Roosevelt, it happened, ruled in a time of relative quiet. Even then he made mistakes. He made perhaps his worst mistakes, though he endeavored to be moral and informed, when his power was least restrained — mistakes possibly more of principle than of policy, but mistakes about which Americans since have often been ashamed: the episode in Panama for one, or the criminal libel suit against Pulitzer for his misinterpretation of that episode. During the last years of his life, after his power was gone, Roosevelt exhibited the characteristics that least became him, prejudices of mind and traits of personality that he had subdued while he felt the responsibilities of office. In office in time of turmoil he might not have conquered them. So too with any man. But Roosevelt especially may have benefited from the limits on Presidential power which men who understood the problem in 1787 created. When he had to proceed with sensitivity for the constitutional balances to his power, the will of Congress and of the courts — or, indeed, for the institutional balances within his party — Roosevelt's performance was noteworthy. Then he demonstrated perception, knowledge, principle of a kind, energy tempered with restraint.

Consolidation, administration, stability — for these he used his power, but they turned on power itself, and power, while it must be, must not be all. This Roosevelt's foreign policy, which next deserves attention, also suggested. Coming back to the beginning, perhaps power particularly must not be all when it promises hard work, duty, order, morality — even welfare — but never mentions happiness. There was strength in Roosevelt's structure and potential for contentment, but in chancing very little, his order risked too much. The wonder is, intrepid though he was, that he never really knew this.

Chapter V I I I

CONCERTS OF POWER

The course of the nineteenth century after Waterloo fostered among the American people, susceptible as they also were to the persuasions of their predispositions, two grand illusions — one that the United States, self-insulated, could avoid involvement in the affairs of the world; another that peace, or at least the absence of war, was a normal condition. To these chimeras, now vanished, Theodore Roosevelt never fell victim. Not strenuosity and bellicosity alone, but a realization of the oneness of the world including the United States, impelled him to insist that the nation recognize its international obligations and keep in readiness sufficient mobilized resources to honor them. The changes in transportation, communication, and production that had altered life in America, Roosevelt understood, altered no less the relations of nations. Internationally as domestically, these changes, he believed, created a situation of potential chaos in which only the availability of power and, when necessary, the application of force could provide the indispensable instruments for a tolerable equilibrium.

Unwilling supinely to commit the direction of American policy to the will of other nations, he depended — in the absence of any generally accepted international law and of any properly constituted and authoritative agency to enforce it — upon the power of the United States. To mobilize that power, with tedious repetition for twenty years he pressed upon his reluctant countrymen the importance of preparedness. This was not simple militarism. Preparedness, as Roosevelt preached it, rested upon a foundation of physical strength: preserved and developed natural resources, a large — indeed an increasing — population, and maximal industrial productivity. To this he added moral resources, especially for women the desire to bear children and for men those inevitable attributes of proper male character, of "the right stuff," such as the renunciation of ease, the capacity to fight, the willingness to sacrifice life. Ultimately of course preparedness involved the military services, their organization, their size, their equipment, and their control by expert general staffs. "It is impossible to treat our foreign policy . . . ," he instructed Congress in a characteristic admonition, "save as conditioned upon the attitude we are willing to take toward our army, and especially toward our navy . . . it is contemptible, for a nation, as for an individual, to . . . proclaim its purposes, or to take positions which are ridiculous if unsupported by potential force, and then to refuse to provide this force."

This dictum, so intimately associated with Theodore Roosevelt, and its good sense, now so laboriously demonstrated by two hot wars and one cold, left unresolved the portentous problem of using whatever force might be prepared. For this Roosevelt had his solution. Encumbered though it unhappily was by moralistic platitudes prodigiously repeated, his foreign policy advanced realistic principles. Often with vulgar brag he recalled confounding sovereigns he had scarcely cautioned. During and after his Presidency, in order to win this point or defend that position, he varied the postures that he struck. But these exaggerations of incidents and accommodations to the immediate did not distort the basic nature of his policy. Beneath his turgid explanations of his conduct, beneath this *démarche* and that detail of his diplomatic ventures, his purpose remained governed — as it clearly was domestically — by those related constants: his quest for order, his faith in power.

He took as his first objective the self-interest of the United States. To this he gave in part strategic definition. National defense, Roosevelt agreed with Admiral Mahan, demanded control of the Caribbean, of the approaches to an isthmian canal, of the ocean triangle with apexes at Panama, Hawaii, and Alaska. But this area, he knew, was not self-contained. The nation had commitments across both oceans. If some of these could be curtailed by retreat — by 1912 he preferred surrendering the Philippines to retaining them with an inadequate defense — there could nevertheless be no inoculation from the East or from the West. In the closing years of the nineteenth century the German fleet pestered Dewey at Manila; the capitals of Europe restrained Japan in China and frowned upon American seizures of so much that had been Spain's; every great power in three continents joined to spank the Boxers. Sooner or later a large disturbance anywhere would touch the United States. Self-interest, then, involved concern for every section of the globe.

Indisputably this concern pleased Roosevelt. He savored entrances upon a vast, well-lighted stage. In any hour he liked to strut. The possibilities of war that caused even the brave to pray stirred in his heart a disquieting delight. These dreadful temperamental traits, however, made his understanding of national interest no less sure. Long before the First World War he accepted the inexorable logic of things international as they had become. "More and more," Roosevelt in 1902 declared to Congress, "the increasing interdependence and complexity of international political and economic relations render it incumbent on all civilized and orderly powers to insist on the proper policing of the world."

This was to be the basis of the Roosevelt corollary. Like the Monroe Doctrine which it emphatically amended, it pertained to the policy of the United States not only in the Americas but also — implicitly — in other parts of the world. Near home, the nation by the new standard would be more jealous and more active than before; abroad, more interested and more involved. Roosevelt declared himself for order and for participation. He practiced what he promised.

In the Caribbean Roosevelt gave his corollary its most specific and its largest application. The background is familiar. Small states washed by that sensuous sea had borrowed in Europe and in the United States funds which their prodigal rulers lacked means or intention to repay. Against Venezuela, a prime offender, Germany and Great Britain, later joined by Italy, in 1902 established a blockade in order to force collection of the debts due their nationals. Venezuela, quickly capitulating, accepted their demand for arbitration. The episode, as Roosevelt saw it, violated an area of primary strategic importance. In time he persuaded himself that by an ultimatum he had scared the Kaiser off. Certainly he wished he had, but there is no good evidence for his claim. After the fact, however, he did announce that preventive intervention by the United States would for the future make unnecessary the kind of intercession that had occurred. By keeping order in the Caribbean he would keep Europe home. "If a nation shows that it knows how to act with reasonable efficiency and decency in social and political matters, if it keeps order and pays its obligations," he explained to Congress in 1904 and again in different words in 1905 — on both occasions for the ears of all the world — "it need fear no interference from the United States. Chronic wrong-doing, or an impotence which results in a general loosening of the ties of civilized society, may in America, as elsewhere, ultimately require intervention by some civilized nation, and in the western hemisphere the adherence of the United States to the Monroe Doctrine may force the United States, however reluctantly, in flagrant cases of such wrong-doing or impotence, to the exercise of an international police power . . . every nation, whether in America or anywhere else, which desires to maintain its freedom, its independence, must ultimately realize that the right of such independence cannot be separated from the responsibility of making good use of it."

Roosevelt meant exactly what he said. To terminate the exasperating cycle of loan, revolution, and default in Santo Domingo, he had already landed forces there and placed under American control the collection of customs, the only sure source of Dominican revenue and the continuing objective of Dominican insurrectionists. It made no difference, he asserted, whether he had done this as an incident to the development of the Monroe Doctrine or simply to establish order. It was now incumbent on the Senate to ratify the treaty that guaranteed stability. "Under the course taken," he maintained, "stability and order and all the benefits of peace are at last coming to Santo Domingo, danger of foreign intervention has been suspended, and there is at last a prospect that all creditors will get justice . . . If the arrangement is terminated by the failure of the treaty chaos will follow; and if chaos follows, sooner or later this government may be involved in serious difficulties with foreign governments over the island, or else may be forced itself to intervene . . ." The Senate backed and filled; Roosevelt adjusted his demands; in time he got his treaty.

In 1906 his mailed fist disciplined Cuba. Intervening with considerable reluctance during a revolution there, he established a provisional government under American direction. To this mission he was invoked by a Cuban government "powerless to quell" the insurrection; by the Cuban constitution his intercession was permitted. Even without these sanctions he doubtless would have acted as he did. "It was evident," he pointed out, "that chaos was impending, and there was every probability that if steps were not immediately taken by this government to try to restore order the representatives of various European nations in the island would apply to their respective governments for armed intervention . . ." "The United States . . . ," he vouched, "wishes nothing of the Cubans save that they shall be able to preserve order among themselves and therefore to preserve their independence." When — to Roosevelt's genuine relief — this appeared again to be the case, the Yankee proconsuls withdrew.

Insistence upon order in areas of strategic significance had provided Roosevelt, before he announced his corollary, with a warrant for acquiring the canal zone in Panama. Long convinced that an isthmian canal was indispensable for American naval policy, persuaded by the report of the second Walker Commission that Panama was the preferred site for this canal, he had no patience with Colombia's rejection of the treaty providing a suitable right of way. He planned before the Panamanian revolt against Colombia to seize what he desired. For this plan he had prepared an apologia, perhaps compelling and certainly convenient. He used it to justify the course he ultimately took. When in 1903 the Panamanians declared their independence, Roosevelt saw to it that American forces aided the revolt. He at once recognized the new republic. Without this collaboration it could not have long survived. In return he received the controversial right of way, control over the zone through which the United States constructed the canal.

Disorder in so vital an area as the isthmus, Roosevelt then declared as he had planned to, had made essential his treatment of Colombia: "The experience of over half a century has shown Colombia to be utterly incapable of keeping order on the Isthmus . . . The control, in the interest of the commerce and traffic of the whole civilized world, of the means of undisturbed transit across the Isthmus of Panama has become of transcendent importance to the United States. We have repeatedly exercised this control by intervening in the course of domestic dissension . . . the goverment of Colombia, though wholly unable to maintain order on the Isthmus, has nevertheless declined to ratify a treaty the conclusion of which opened the only chance to secure its own stability and to guarantee permanent peace on, and the construction of a canal across, the Isthmus." Under these circumstances, he averred, the United States had no choice but to aid the revolution. This reasoning was not merely a cloak for grabbing land. In what he did, certainly in the way he did it, Roosevelt was wrong; but he was also convinced and consistent. In Panama as in Cuba and Santo Domingo, he used power to establish order. Had he been elected President in 1912, in order to protect American lives and property he would "have restored order in Mexico, if necessary at the cost of war."

This was imperialism — about that there can be no argument.

In proximate areas of strategic significance a powerful nation interceded by force, assumed local administrative functions, and according to its own rather than to indigenous criteria imposed order from above. This for Roosevelt was also the function of government within the United States and, significantly, for powerful and stable governments throughout the world. Again and again in corresponding with his British friends he drew attention to the similarity of England's mission in Egypt and America's in Panama. The burden did not fall upon the white man alone. The Western powers, he believed, had obligations to preserve domestic peace in China; the United States, of course, had special duties in the Philippines; the British, in India. But it was Japan that he expected especially to police the Orient. He hoped that from her example China in time would learn self-government. The Yellow Sea he saw as Japan's Caribbean. Korea he acknowledged to be her charge. "I should like to see Japan have Korea . . . ," he wrote a German confidant in 1900; "she deserves it for what she has done." The Japanese violation of the treaty guaranteeing Korean independence Roosevelt, while President, specifically approved. "Korea," he later asserted, "is absolutely Japan's. To be sure, by treaty it was solemnly covenanted that Korea should remain independent. But Korea was itself helpless to enforce the treaty, and it was out of the question to suppose that any other nation . . . would attempt to do for the Koreans what they were utterly unable to do for themselves. Moreover, the treaty rested on the false assumption that Korea could govern herself well . . . Japan could not afford to see Korea in the hands of a great foreign power . . . Therefore, when Japan thought the right time had come, it calmly tore up the treaty and took Korea . . ." Japan's work in Korea, Roosevelt suggested, was "like that done under similar conditions by the chief colonial administrators of the United States, England, France, and Germany . . . The Japanese have restored and enforced order, built roads and railways, carried out great engineering works, introduced modern sanitation . . . [and] a modern school system,

and doubled the commerce and the agricultural output . . ."
Roosevelt applauded. "For the interest of all the world . . . ,"
he had long believed, "each part of the world should be prosperous and well policed . . ."

The international police power that Roosevelt advocated was
not to be used against prosperous and stable nations, whatever
their size or strength. Specifically exempting Argentina, Brazil
and Chile from the application of his corollary, Roosevelt referred
to their safekeeping the stability of America below the bulge.
Similarly, aggression by one of the qualified constabulary against
another could not be charged off to the police. Such action, producing as it did mammoth disorder, Roosevelt would not by any
token justify. "Korea's case," he maintained heatedly when Germany began her march of conquest, "afforded not the slightest
analogy to Belgium's . . ." It was not the "scrap of paper" that so
much disturbed him, but the Kaiser's gross violation of the peace.
Agents of chaos, the Germans were by force to be controlled. For
this he advocated American support to the Allies. Earlier he had
attempted within the limits of his influence to achieve balances
of force that might at once ensure the interests of the United
States and dissuade would-be disrupters of world order.

Relying on and using power as he did at home and in proconsulships, Roosevelt accepted power as a legitimate, and the
controlling, element in the relations among major nations. Always
with confidence and generally with control he manipulated what
power he had. There were unhappy episodes. However right his
law and geography may have been, his rude and threatening
attitude about the Alaskan boundary unnecessarily offended Canada. He overestimated his achievements. No international crisis
he helped resolve compared in magnitude with his description of
it. But he was not, his critics to the contrary, either a reckless fool
or a naïve tool of London or Berlin. He understood the nature
of the rivalries that beset the world, estimated accurately the
existing and prospective might of the contestants — their designs
and limitations — evaluated knowingly America's involvements

and advantage, and with all this in mind adroitly shifted weights to preserve in Europe and gain in Asia equilibriums tolerable to the United States.

Europe during Roosevelt's Presidency on only one occasion caused him much alarm. The balance of European power as it existed at the turn of the century he found acceptable. There was no challenge to American strategic or economic interests, there was no unchecked danger to the general peace. Of England Roosevelt cherished fondest thoughts. Grateful for the Pax Britannica and for her growing friendship, he could not contemplate a war between the English-speaking peoples. Judging on the bases of size, resources and location, he considered Russia potentially the foremost European power. Decay and despotism, he felt, for the time immobilized her, but for later generations, he predicted, she would be a "serious problem." Had the Kaiser "had the 'instinct for the jugular,'" Roosevelt maintained, he would have kept most careful guard on Russia. As it was, he realized that Germany looked with at least equal suspicion on France and England. But Roosevelt did not believe that Britain would or France could elect aggression, and until the last months of his term as President he scoffed at England's fears of Germany. Then he admitted to a British friend that Germany, at any rate the Kaiser, might entertain "red dreams of glory," but these might be dispelled. He had assisted earlier in preserving that monarch's uncertain sense of reasonable portions.

On that occasion German jealousy of French hegemony in North Africa imperiled European peace. Aware as he was of nationalistic tensions and of the developing network of alliances, Roosevelt appreciated the severity of the crisis of 1905 over Morocco. Because the United States had no immediate interests in Morocco, he did not care about the detailed claims of the powers to that land. He cared that these claims be settled peacefully, however, for in the peaceful status quo of Europe, he realized, the United States had large concern. Overcoming his disinclination to appear a "Meddlesome Mattie," Roosevelt at the request of the Kaiser urged France and Britain to negotiate. They agreed, as they probably would have had he not interceded. The United States, although represented at the ensuing conference at Algeciras, little affected its outcome. Roosevelt's role was small. But it was useful. More important, by acting promptly and vigorously as he did, he demonstrated to Europe and to the American people that the President of the United States recognized the stake of the United States in any European crisis. In this public recognition, rather than in any of its products, his reputation was secure.

Roosevelt played a larger role in Asia. In the power situation there, he judged, slumbering China was of no account, but to prevent dislocations of power he valued the prevailing fiction of her territorial integrity. To stabilize the Orient he relied primarily upon a balance between Russia and Japan. During his Presidency this trembled. When in 1904 the Russo-Japanese War began, Roosevelt brooded over its "immense possibilities . . . for the future." A Russian triumph, he concluded, would be "a blow to civilization," but "her destruction as an eastern Asiatic power would also . . . be unfortunate. It is best that she should be left face to face with Japan so that each may have a moderative action on the other." Officially neutral, Roosevelt at first sympathized with Japan, supposedly the weaker belligerent. He later asserted that he warned Germany and France that should they combine against Japan, he would "proceed to whatever length was necessary on her behalf." This warning, which was unnecessary, he never issued, but his prevarication doubtless had some basis in his unexpressed intentions.

The progress of the war, revealing Russia's unexpected impotence, changed Roosevelt's initial bias. Victorious on land and sea, Japan seemed capable, at large expense of men and money, of driving deep into Siberia. This would have produced precisely the imbalance Roosevelt feared. He was therefore particularly pleased to serve, at the request of both belligerents, as peacemaker. In that capacity he urged upon them both — Russia, flaccid but still proud, immense and stubborn; Japan, confident, ravenous, but very near exhaustion — the necessity for reasonableness. The Treaty of Portsmouth which he helped so greatly to negotiate disappointed the Japanese who had come to expect a large indemnity they did not receive. For this they came inordinately to blame Roosevelt and the United States. But the treaty, eminently equitable, accomplished Roosevelt's purpose. It restored peace. It preserved balance. "Each power," he reported with unconcealed satisfaction, "will be in a sense the guarantor of the other's good conduct."

The guarantee was anything but absolute. Entangled as she was in European alliances, nourishing as she did ambitions both in central and in eastern Asia, Russia alone or consorting with the Germans or the French might yet endeavor to redeem her losses. "There is no nation in the world," Roosevelt remarked, "which, more than Russia, holds in its hands the fate of the coming years . . ." To bend that fate he approved "entirely" the Anglo-Japanese alliance. Advantageous to the peace of Asia, it did not, he believed, endanger the United States, for "beyond any other two powers" he expected England and the United States to continue to be friendly. He was less sure about Japan. Emboldened by her victory, infested with the Samurai spirit, Japan might possibly "enter into a general career of insolence and aggression" which would be "unpleasant." The best preventive, he maintained, was American power, particularly the navy. As Russia balanced Japan in eastern Asia, so could the United States in the Pacific.

Especially to Japan Roosevelt spoke softly; especially for her view he displayed his biggest stick. The talking pertained to immigration. Race prejudice, resentment of coolie labor, reprehensible prattle of a yellow peril provoked on the West Coast discriminations against the Japanese and their descendants who had settled there, attacks on their persons and property, and demands for the cessation of Oriental immigration. This of course distressed the Japanese who, with understandable sensitivity, particularly objected to any governmental action that made their emigrants seem less desirable than those from western nations. Mannered but firm, Roosevelt relieved this pass. His intercession decreased existing and blocked impending discrimination in California. His Secretary of State arranged the Gentlemen's Agreement which, without insulting the Japanese, effectively checked coolie immigration. At the same time Roosevelt made it clear to Japan that immigration policy was a domestic matter, subject to international discussion but to be settled by national decision.

He also bared his fist. During the crisis over immigration, the indignation of the Japanese, revealed in their press and in public demonstrations, falsely persuaded many Americans and some European observers that war was near. Roosevelt received alarmed reports of Japanese fifth columns in Hawaii and of troops, disguised as laborers, in Mexico. These he properly discounted. But while he did not believe the Japanese were planning war, he proposed to take no chances. With special fervor he advanced his naval program. Both as a device to train and test the fleet and as a warning to Japan, he sent his battleships, his fleet in being, to the Pacific, across that ocean and then around the world. He had detected, he recalled, "a very, very slight undertone of veiled truculence" in Japan's communications; he had concluded that they thought he was afraid of them. "I am more concerned over this Japanese situation than almost any other," he confessed to Root. "Thank Heaven we have the navy in good shape. It is high time, however, that it should go on a cruise around the world . . . it will have a pacific effect to show that it can be done . . ."

"It was essential that we should have it clearly understood," Roosevelt explained in his autobiography, "by our own people especially, but also by other peoples, that the Pacific was as much our home waters as the Atlantic . . ." At each port of call the fleet observed the niceties of peaceful protocol. Especially in Japan its welcome was effusive. These courtesies, however, did not hide Roosevelt's purpose. His show of force reminded Japan of one check upon her power. This, he believed, for the while confined temptations she may have felt for insolent aggression. "The most important service that I rendered to peace," he concluded, probably correctly, "was the voyage of the battle fleet round the world."

So it was that Roosevelt sought security and peace in concerts of power in Europe and Asia and in power applied to discipline disorder. His was not a legalistic system. Nation states themselves decided, as they interpreted their interests, how best to canalize their force. Although from each he hoped for courteous restraint, to ensure that quality he relied not upon a world league or laws but upon consciousness by each great nation of counterbalanced power. Where the power situation was reliable and well defined, disputes of small proportions, he believed, were susceptible to arbitration; he negotiated treaties of arbitration that deliberately excluded the kinds of differences that ordinarily caused war. In some remote future, he grudgingly allowed, power might be internationalized; accepting the Nobel Prize for Peace, later during World War I, he advocated an "international posse comitatus." But even then he viewed this as a distant dream that only sentimentalists considered pertinent to policy. "As yet there is no likelihood," he maintained in 1906, stating then a position from which he never really departed, "of establishing any kind of international power . . . which can effectively check wrong-doing, and in these circumstances it would be both a foolish and an evil thing for a great and free nation to deprive itself of the power to protect its own rights and even in exceptional cases to stand up for the rights of others. Nothing would more promote iniquity, . . . than for the free and enlightened peoples . . . deliberately to render themselves powerless while leaving every despotism and barbarism armed . . . The chance for the settlement of disputes peacefully . . . now depends mainly upon the possession by the nations that mean to do right of sufficient armed strength to make their purpose effective."

As ever he tended to equate right with order and to make order the province of self-restrained power. This left no room for arbitration or international conventions except about the relatively trivial or between most trusting friends. In criticizing the foreign policies of his successors, Roosevelt made his own position emphatically clear. By failing in any manner to chastise Germany after her violations of the Hague Conventions which the United States had signed, the Wilson Administration — Roosevelt asserted — demonstrated that without mobilized power, vigorously applied, those conventions, like the peace treaties negotiated by Bryan, meant nothing. Power — not paper — prevailed. Roosevelt had earlier condemned with revelatory candor the treaties of arbitration proposed by Taft. "I have no sympathy with . . . [the] arbitration treaty business," Roosevelt declared to a British intimate. "If we were avowedly to limit it to a treaty between Great Britain and ourselves I should say Yes with all heartiness . . . But as a model for world treaties, for treaties between us or you and every other nation, I think it is absurd. I do not think it would do great damage simply because the purpose which the worthy peace disciple of the Carnegie type has embodied in it would not be carried out in practice. But this would mean hypocrisy, and hypocrisy is not nice. If the purpose nominally contained in this treaty were lived up to, and arbitration had been resorted to for the last thirty years, England would not now be in Egypt, . . . to the great detriment not merely of England, but of Egypt . . . ; and Cuba would still be Spanish, and the Isthmus of Panama would belong to Colombia, and the canal would not be even begun . . . The whole business is tainted by that noxious form of silliness which always accompanies the sentimental refusal to look facts in the face."

Words such as these, so glibly spoken, damned much of Roosevelt's point of view. He confessed, after all, that there was a standard his objectives violated. He called it sentimental. With more experience, the western world has learned to call it nicer names. If, as Roosevelt judged, its application was remote, nevertheless it had, to be applied at all, first to be defined and then by power, such as England had in Egypt and the United States in Panama, to be honored. The conclusion once again imperiously suggests itself that Roosevelt did not want to be controlled — not, obviously, by a body of law interpreted by arbitration; nor, as it happened, in foreign policy as in domestic policy, by Congress.

The latter he also freely admitted. "In domestic politics," Roosevelt held, "Congress in the long run is apt to do what is right. It is in foreign politics, and in preparing the army and navy that we are apt to have most difficulty, because these are just the subjects as to which the average American citizen does not take the trouble to think carefully or deeply." Both Congress and the people, he complained, had been "utterly indifferent" to such work of his as that in Santo Domingo. A free people, learning only by experience, he concluded, hesitated to accept the judgment even of those it trusted most. It was therefore a great misfortune for free government when it lacked "a great leader, a practical, powerful man who cares with all his heart for the game." This kind of man he tried to be. Without reference to public opinion or to the Congress, after only private, unofficial consultation, he initiated the two episodes of his foreign policy he most exalted. Proudly he recalled dispatching the fleet around the world: "I determined on the move without consulting the Cabinet, precisely as I took Panama without consulting the Cabinet. A council of war never fights, and in a crisis the duty of a leader is to lead . . ."

When this was said it probably needed saying. The President, better informed than Congress about foreign affairs, more capable of prompt action, must have large freedom to act alone. Roosevelt, however, in emphasizing this, overlooked some limiting considerations. It was, to begin with, his own impetuosity and stubbornness that often blinded him to the constitutional basis for the conduct of foreign policy. And because the consequences to individuals of foreign policy are particularly invulnerable to legal review or compensation, those affected adversely by uninhibited use of Presidential power over foreign affairs have inadequate redress. Some congressional participation in such decision-making is therefore especially important. It is also important because without it even the most conscientious steward of the people may less accurately interpret their desires. Misinterpretation can initiate commitments from which an unwilling people may, possibly with embarrassing results, force government to retreat. As much by chance as by design, Roosevelt escaped these dangers. None of his foreign policies seriously jeopardized the immediate interest of any substantial number of Americans. In every case, after he had acted popular opinion by and large supported what he had done. He understood, furthermore, so much better than did his countrymen the inescapable involvements of the United States that what he did was perhaps enough worth doing to have been worth doing less than well. Had he had power in other times, however — in 1897 or in 1915 — these redemptions need not have pertained. Judging by his opinions at those crucial hours, he might have gone too far, too fast, too flagrantly.

Nor was self-restraint, according to criteria of his own or later times, sufficient check on Roosevelt. Although he discovered always in his foreign policy the moral and the just, others did not. There was, to be sure, much of the sentimental in those of his contemporaries who questioned his taking of Panama and his intercession in Santo Domingo. There was also considerable good sense. The peoples on whom imperialistic orders were imposed needed to be helped but deserved, they felt, to be consulted. Roosevelt's ambitions and impatience, like those of other western leaders, at sword's point sowed the seeds of wild winds Point Four may never tame. So too with balanced power: the world, as Roosevelt knew, had no effective legal system; the time for disarmament was far away; the "peace of righteousness" depended for the while on force alerted. But Roosevelt always backed away from making righteousness a collective duty. "I am insisting," he asserted shortly before he died, "upon Nationalism as against Internationalism. I am for saying with a bland smile whatever Nationalism demands." Considering the nation or the nation in alliance as the effective and appropriate unit of conscience, he resisted making power responsible to the consensus of a community large enough to contain potential dissenters. He recognized too little the need at least to attempt to develop rules according to which such a community could live, rules whose infractions such a community collectively would punish. Lacking this, justice and morality and righteousness meant nothing except by his own definition, a measure too subject to convenient intuition, too vague, too fallible to satisfy for long even his fellow Americans. The awful suspicion ever lingered that he cared as much for fighting as for right.

Nevertheless he discerned some permanently useful principles. The duty of a leader is to lead — perhaps especially in foreign policy. The United States is part of an interdependent world. If the use of force in international society has limitations, it also has legitimate capacities. Without force, the best intentions fail to stop destruction. On this belief Roosevelt based much of his postpresidential activity — the subject next to be explored. Moreover, as he realized, deploying restricted force with full vigor in small situations of turmoil may confine turbulence. If sometimes he selected improper situations, he did attempt humanely to control the use of force and to make terminal his disciplinary engagements. Power, as he judged, is a present element in the conduct of world affairs. This being so, the rulers of the nation must be prepared, as Roosevelt was, constantly and unashamed to venture power politics. On this, well done, depends American security and possibly the prevention of another total war.

Chapter I X

"... AND BY OPPOSING END THEM"

"*Even in America,*" Henry Adams once suggested, "the Indian Summer of life should be a little sunny and a little sad, like the season, and infinite in wealth and depth of tone — but never hustled." Such a season Theodore Roosevelt never knew. He could not. Always his energy found crags for him to climb. So of a quiet afternoon while President he raced some titled diplomat through Rock Creek Park. So, leaving high office intending to retire from public life when only fifty, he trailed game through Africa, then moved safari to Rome where he argued with the papacy, to Berlin where he chaffed the Kaiser's manners, to London where he helped to bury one king and to lecture others. Returning home, greeted like a hero, he found a sea of troubles. These were real. During the remainder of his life a succession of them threatened the things he held important — his party, his policies of government, his doctrines of international behavior. He would probably have made compelling troubles of his own had they not existed. As it was, the hero did not have to contrive. Persuaded by convictions, restless, driven by his endless need for power, he took arms at once, never to retire. Of course he mobilized his hosts.

He also erred. The extravagance with which he championed proper principles beclouded their merit and vitiated his strength. The savageness he permitted himself to feel destroyed his judgment about men, about policy, about the instruments of politics he understood so well. Perhaps only such an African buffalo as killed one brother of Grey of Fallodon or such a lion as killed another could have provided Roosevelt with the kinder fate he seemed to seek. But the beasts did not overcome him and he failed to pacify himself. *Hubris* conquered. This was tragedy.

Inexorably out of Roosevelt's past it developed. The continua in his activities after he returned from Europe were as considerable as were his aberrations. He was determined to do good. He quickly concluded, as he always had before, that he could labor for the right only through politics. Once embroiled again in politics, he endeavored at first to find and hold a middle position, to adjust to local situations, and to forward the policies he had long supported. But these objectives proved to be no longer compatible, for in the year that Roosevelt was away, President Taft and the Republican left wing in Congress had moved so far apart on such issues as the tariff, conservation, and railroad regulation that no man or platform could in 1910 bring them comfortably together again.

Roosevelt was engaged in politics almost as soon as he arrived in New York. Disenchanted congressional Republicans sought solace and political assistance in Oyster Bay where they continually regaled the attentive ex-President with emphatic accounts of his successor's alleged apostasies. Governor Hughes of New York persuaded Roosevelt to join him in opposition to local Republican powers whose support Taft needed. Local situations elsewhere, involving as they did ideological differences at once induced and enhanced by an overt struggle for control of the party machinery, aroused Roosevelt's interests and loyalties. Responding to the stimuli that had conditioned his entire adult life, he returned during the primary and election campaigns of 1910 to the hustings which his heart had never left.

His ideas and his tactics were familiar. Addressing himself in articles and speeches to public questions, both domestic and international, he clarified and amplified his Presidential doctrines on consolidation, stability, and administration, adding nothing except a title — *The New Nationalism*. "I am not trying to be subtle or original," he explained. "I am trying to make the plain everyday citizen . . . stand for the things which I regard as essential to good government." Frequently on this characteristic account attacking measures with which Taft was identified, he revealed the restlessness that was to become revolt. But throughout 1910, at the New York State Convention, campaigning in the South and West, and in his private letters, Roosevelt — still a regular — supported Taft. Condemning the ultradissenters as vigorously as he condemned the ultra-Taft men, he called one of Taft's most ardent detractors a goose, another a lunatic; and he praised the President moderately but often. It was clear that Taft had not met Roosevelt's expectations, but it was equally clear that he still considered Taft to be the logical candidate for 1912.

Weaving down the middle of the road, Roosevelt adjusted to local exigencies. In New York State he endorsed the Payne-Aldrich Tariff, the party's controversial new vehicle of protection, so bitterly resented by the Western Republican insurgents. In Indiana and elsewhere he disowned the tariff. Possibly this weakened his appeals for the Republican ticket; in any case most of the candidates he favored lost either in their primaries or to their Democratic rivals. But his performance, whatever its liabilities, conformed to the ambivalence toward the tariff and to the opportunism on local politics which had characterized his Presidential successes. The times, intense with political feeling, had changed more than had Roosevelt.

But the greatest change for Roosevelt, as he realized increasingly, was in his role. He still had a following of plain people and of politicians, but he had no power. He could beseech and denounce; he could not appoint or discharge. No longer head of the party, he could not command even a precinct committee; no longer President, he could not even attempt to manage Congress. In 1910 he performed as a delegate to a convention or as an auxiliary speaker in a campaign. In spite of his prestige, he failed in those unfamiliar and frustrating roles to add winning strength to the candidacies of men whose talents he regarded highly. Because of his prestige, he may even have hurt them by attracting to himself publicity they needed. Still concerned with realizable ideals, still convinced that their realization had to come through politics, he learned again how difficult was politics without power.

He relearned also that power attracts power. Many of the informed or masterful politicians and industrialists upon whom Roosevelt had often relied for advice now talked more often to the new President. Taft, not Roosevelt, could most readily employ their services or serve their interests. The councils at Oyster Bay therefore contained a disproportionate number of critics or malcontents, too few policy-makers, too many observers. Roosevelt accepted them partly because he was from the first emotionally prepared to resent any successor, partly because he needed to dominate some court. He became, however, their victim as well as their master, for their presence and their counsel more and more shut him off from communication with the intelligences who had helped him use his power, the men who tried but failed to prevent his ultimate decision to challenge the political system he had once managed.

Taft himself should have prevented this. While Roosevelt had some faith in the political power of an aroused people, a faith perhaps exaggerated by his reception in New York and by the reports of the insurgents, he had demonstrably an equal, probably a greater faith in the political power of the party organization. Taft might have exploited this, might have laid down the law to Roosevelt as Roosevelt had to Hanna. But Taft neither asserted himself nor made clear his anxieties. He sulked. In dealing with his Congress he had succumbed so much to Aldrich and Cannon that he lost the confidence of the Republican left. In dealing with Roosevelt, he yielded too much to the spinsters of his palace, to an ambitious secretary, a suspicious wife, and unimaginative politicos. Reflecting their pettiness, he came to take spiteful pleasure in Roosevelt's embarrassments. Sharing their uncertainties, he did not in time discipline his former chief and potential rival. A stronger or a bolder man might have held the wings of the party together, as Roosevelt had, or, failing that, at least discouraged competition.

For some time after the Democratic victories of 1910 Roosevelt was discouraged, not by Taft, but by what appeared to be a popular repudiation of his efforts. Although he continued in his columns in *The Outlook* to criticize administration policies, in politics he seemed to be in tired equilibrium. He refused to be associated with the movement among anti-Taft Republicans to nominate Senator La Follette in 1912. He exchanged with Taft a series of cautiously cordial letters about the Japanese problem in California. "An ex-President is not in a very comfortable position," Roosevelt lamented to a western friend. "The easy thing for him to do is to say that he will do nothing, and will have nothing to say about any public movement; and next to this, the easy thing is to write in a way that will deprive his writings of all effect. Moreover, besides being the easy thing, there are genuine arguments that could be advanced to show that the first of these positions is the proper out to take, and that an ex-President does not do enough good to counterbalance the disadvantages of his taking any part as regards public questions."

This attitude could not persist. Gradually during 1911 Roosevelt resolved to take arms again. Three of Taft's policies especially aroused him: the treaties of arbitration which the President negotiated violated Roosevelt's conceptions of the proper bases for the conduct of foreign policy; the President's administration of Alaskan public lands reversed — as had some of his earlier decisions — Roosevelt's program for the conservation and use of natural resources; Taft's antitrust suits against the United States Steel Corporation and the International Harvester Company and his approval of the Supreme Court's reasoning in the American Tobacco and Standard Oil cases contradicted Roosevelt's opinion on industrial consolidation and control. Fixing on these issues, for so long among his central concerns, Roosevelt publicly and unsparingly attacked his successor. The two stopped corresponding.

Meanwhile other seeds of trouble grew. Many of the disenchanted, despairing of nominating La Follette in place of Taft, coaxed Roosevelt to be a candidate. The incubus of Taft, they argued, not Roosevelt's intercession, had damaged the campaign of 1910. Of available Republicans, they insisted, Roosevelt alone enjoyed the confidence of the people; only he could reunite and save the party; only he could supervise a program of intelligent reform. All of this Roosevelt was ready to believe; some of it was true. Without prompting, furthermore, he considered La Follette politically weak and intellectually unsound. And his loyalty to Taft fast faded. Before 1910 the President had forced out of public service men Roosevelt both trusted and befriended; after 1910, endeavoring to punish the insurgents and build his own strength for nomination, Taft replaced a corps of lesser government officials, some of them Roosevelt's former agents, all his suppliants for revenge. These and other politicians, business leaders offended by Taft's policies, disinterested citizens who felt the President had associated with reaction dispatched to Oyster Bay a volume of entreating mail that struck the eager Roosevelt as the people calling.

This pressure and his irritations by the end of 1911 closed Roosevelt's mind to caution. He would, he concluded, accept the Presidential nomination if the people wanted him. In a letter of January 1912 he announced his availability. Immediately before and after this disclosure, Roosevelt's intimates implored him to reconsider. From a receptive posture he would be forced, Root warned him, into an aggressive one. This would destroy the party. William Loeb, Roosevelt's secretary during his Presidential years, agreed. Sit out 1912, he counseled; let Taft be nominated and defeated; return in 1916. Others reiterated this advice. To all Roosevelt insisted that he must abide the decision of the people. To some he privately confessed his pique with Taft. To himself he may have admitted, though he probably did not, that in 1912 — as in 1904 when he conquered and in 1908 when he painfully withdrew — he wanted desperately to be President.

Root was right. Roosevelt soon provided amplifiers for the people's voice. He arranged to have a group of progressive Republican governors petition him to run. Shortly thereafter his working hat was in the ring. Then he and Taft began their acerbic campaign for nomination. Their differences as they stumped pertained less and less to issues and more and more to personalities and power. Arraigning each other heatedly, the old friends wounded themselves, their good names, and the party for which they struggled.

From the start Roosevelt was preferred not only by the more progressive faction of party regulars but also by a majority of Republicans. This was partly because of his enduring personal appeal. It was also because he intensified the tone of his protest. While his progressivism still derived from his feelings about order in an industrial society, he embraced for the season the current, popular panaceas of political democracy, endorsing with limited reservations the initiative, referendum, recall of judicial decisions, and the extension of direct primaries.

His focus on the last had indispensable strategic importance. To overcome Taft's control of the Republican machinery for selecting delegates to the national convention, Roosevelt and his supporters endeavored to establish by local legislation in as many states as possible a Presidential primary. Among those states where such a primary was used, Roosevelt delegates won a majority of seats and Roosevelt accumulated an impressive plurality. Elsewhere, however, Taft's agents by and large manipulated the machinery they controlled to elect Taft delegates. The Rooseveltians again and again contested these contrived elections. Although their contests had little legal validity, they pursued them with fanatic moral fervor. Taft, to be sure, turning his back to the party's rank and file, was putting his nomination above the party's chances for success in November, but in a struggle for power this is a fairly standard political response. And for all his myopia, Taft, breaking few rules or precedents, was managing the party by devices Roosevelt had employed in 1904 and 1908.

Yet Roosevelt, recognizing the weaknesses of his organization, sure of his own righteousness, flattered by his pluralities, and consumed with desire for office, believed and preached that Taft was stealing the nomination.

Taft succeeded. His agents on the national committee settled the contests at issue in his favor. Obviously he controlled the convention. Taft knew that he had won with ruthlessness, but he felt his triumph was legitimate. Inflamed by their own vituperation, neither he nor Roosevelt seriously considered compromising on some third candidate. And Roosevelt, convinced that Bourbon fraud alone had stopped him, ordered his substantial bloc of delegates to walk out. At his command they bolted. By his hands he shattered the institution to which he had devoted his professional life. By his choice he abandoned the techniques of political behavior in which he had excelled, the principles of political comportment he had made robust. Invoking the Eighth Commandment, he stood, he said, at Armageddon and he battled for the Lord; he heard his hosts sing Christian hymns of confirmation; his leonine spirit soared in moral triumph. And yet he knew, as he set out to construct a new party — the platform for his candidacy — that he could not hope to win, that his contumacy made a Democrat the President, that for the while he could salvage neither policies nor power — only pride.

The Progressive party — Roosevelt's creature — was a politician's Gothic horror. Composed primarily of disgruntled Republicans, it won the allegiance of a segment of do-good reformers who confused it with the ark of the covenant, a bevy of men of wealth who sponsored it partly because they shared Roosevelt's opinion on consolidation, partly because they hoped for a new career of power in politics, a rank and file of middle-class men of good will who had either tired of Taft or who worshipped Roosevelt, a tiny corps of bold intelligences who took the long chance of making the new party a permanent national organization, and a handful of professionals who used it to further their personal or local interests. It attracted very few professionals of parts, even among progressives, for bolting, such men realized as Roosevelt had in 1884, brings dirty weather. It was a party with only three assets, all transitory: enthusiasm, money, and a Presidential candidate. The enthusiasm and the money vanished with defeat. The candidate understood political organization too well to expect a group of ardent amateurs — even wealthy amateurs — running an incomplete ticket, to provide the stuff of victory in 1912 or continuity thereafter. After the election of Woodrow Wilson, Roosevelt was prepared to dissolve the party he had made as soon as it suited his convenience.

It was not immediately convenient. Although with the passing of each month the party became more and more an army of captains without companies, although gradually even the captains and the colonels departed, returning to the Republican fold or enlisting with the Democrats, the lingering rancor between Republicans and Progressives impeded their overt coöperation. In those states where they had done well, Progressive leaders hesitated to surrender the political power they had acquired. And the national leaders, including Roosevelt, found their party a useful agency for the publicizing of their ideas and an indispensable instrument for negotiating the terms of any reunion. Roosevelt therefore continued to maintain the semblance of continuity, to direct his nucleus of followers in Congress, and to prepare the Progressive congressional and state campaigns of 1914.

His work was arduous. Within the party the advocates of grand reform — in Roosevelt's words "the lunatic fringe" — struggled with the cautious faction recruited from business and finance. In Washington Woodrow Wilson's Democratic Congress lowered the tariff, established the federal reserve system, passed the Clayton Antitrust Act, and created the Federal Trade Commission. Roosevelt could persuade few voters that the refusal of the Democrats to establish a tariff commission or to model the F. T. C. according to Progressive prescriptions detracted significantly from Wilson's achievements. Deprived of a platform, divided and dispirited, the Progressives made a dismal showing in 1914. One critic gibed that the Bull Moose had lapsed into innocuous desuetude. Roosevelt agreed. The only questions that remained were where, when, and how the corpse was to be buried.

Right after the debacle of 1914, Roosevelt and his close advisers cut to a minimum their party's expenses, abandoned its regular publications, and reduced its organizing efforts. There they stopped, for what remained of party structure and of the dwindling ranks of loyal knights of Armageddon provided Roosevelt with just enough leverage to let him hope, as the major parties turned their energies to 1916, that his might once again become a central role.

It took time for his hopes to revive. As late as September 1915, attempting to put aside his world, he wrote the party's national chairman in a plaintive key: "It is perfectly evident to me that this people have made up their minds not only against the policies in which I believe but finally against me personally. The bulk of them are convinced that I am actuated by motives of personal ambition and . . . have not the good of the country at heart." Ambitious Roosevelt was, but he also had always at heart the nation's welfare. The trouble was that by the spring of 1916 he came to identify that welfare with himself, as he always had before. This is a common enough failing. Another Roosevelt repeatedly discovered that he was indispensable. More recently Americans have been assured that what is good for General Motors is good for them. In all such cases, motive is a complicated matter. Theodore Roosevelt in 1916 manifestly coveted the Presidency, but for this he had reasons — some good reasons — beyond his own desire.

As much as anything that Taft had ever done, Woodrow Wilson's foreign policy exasperated Roosevelt. The President's vacillations toward Mexico at once damaged American prestige, engaged American forces in untoward situations, and failed to accomplish his announced objectives. Wilson's attitude toward the war in Europe seemed to Roosevelt even more unhappy. The

President attempted to be neutral, to deal with both the Western and the Central powers according to what he considered established rules for the relations between belligerents and neutrals, and to use American detachment for negotiating peace. Roosevelt on the contrary quickly took sides. The German invasion of Belgium and the German atrocities there, he concluded, deserved swift punishment. He had less use than Wilson did for rules. The President's protests against German submarine warfare he found too mild and inconclusive; after the sinking of the *Lusitania*, attended as it was by the loss of many American lives, Roosevelt would have broken off relations with the Germans — a step Wilson deliberately avoided. And toward peacemaking, except on Franco-British terms, Roosevelt was hostile.

This coolness derived from one terrible conviction, one discerning conclusion. The conviction, which Roosevelt liked to call heroic, he spelled out to an English friend. "I am as nearly sure as can be," he wrote, "that England and France will benefit immensely by the war. Both of them have shown ugly traits at times during the lifetime of the generation that has recently grown to manhood and perhaps it was necessary that their manhood should be tried and purged in the ordeal of this dreadful fiery furnace." As soon as he dared, he proposed this grim ordeal by battle for Americans. The conclusion, never so starkly stated, he suggested in his public speeches and essays. He believed then, as he long had, that a German triumph, by upsetting irremediably the balance of power in Europe, would threaten the security of the United States.

War, then, involved both the strenuous life and safety. Yet good judge of public opinion that he was, Roosevelt did not propose what he clearly desired, that the United States enter the war, until American negotiations with Germany about her submarine policy had failed, until Wilson's careful patience was exhausted. What Roosevelt did demand was first a sterner policy toward Germany, a policy that might have speeded a declaration of war, but perhaps not have aided substantially the Allies' cause. In fact the Allies got from America the things they initially needed most, for Wilson's concepts of neutrality did not preclude the loans and the munitions purchased by those loans which crossed the ocean in spite of German submarines.

Roosevelt also demanded, in keeping with his lifelong principle, that the United States prepare. "If, as an aftermath of this war," he advised, "some great Old World power or combination of powers made war on us . . . , our chance of securing justice would rest exclusively on the efficiency of our fleet and army . . . No arbitration treaties, or peace treaties, . . . no tepid good will of neutral powers, would help us in even the smallest degree. If our fleet were conquered, New York and San Francisco would be seized and probably each would be destroyed as Louvain was destroyed . . ." This made sense. Furthermore, increasing difficulties with Germany over submarine warfare foreshadowed war and made preparedness particularly urgent. Yet Wilson for months complacently ignored the issue. Roosevelt attributed this to physical timidity. Actually the President's timidity was political; he hesitated to advocate a policy so much of his party resisted. When at last he could not avoid speaking out, the President spoke too moderately, recommending belatedly a considerable increase in the navy but not conscription or even a convincing expansion of the regular army. Moreover, he tolerated a Secretary of the Navy and a Secretary of War whose confusion, inattention to industrial preparation, and excessive deference to peacetime mores dangerously retarded the development of the armed services. Possibly Wilson could not have persuaded Congress to do more than it did, but he could have tried and he could have accomplished more himself. The leadership he abandoned, Roosevelt, more than any other man, supplied. His incessant attacks on the Administration's lassitude, while exaggerated, helped to create an essential general awareness of the nation's military inadequacy, to move the President to act, to make possible what was done and make evident how much remained for doing.

Roosevelt's leadership was not all so salutary. Condemning

cultural differences within the country to which he gave distorted emphasis, he preached an intolerantly monistic gospel of Americanism. There were a few German agents in the United States; there were many German sympathizers. But Roosevelt increasingly equated harmless sympathy for Germany, honest neutrality, indeed honest pacifism, with sabotage and sedition; increasingly he interpreted disagreement with his views on foreign and military policy as both timorous and treacherous. Alike about preparedness and Americanism, he spoke out sooner and sharper than not only Wilson but also Taft, Root, and the overwhelming majority of Republicans. Sure of himself, he berated those who lagged. Their loitering, he believed, disqualified them for the responsibilities of highest office. Gradually he concluded that in his hands alone would the nation's fate be safe.

So persuaded, Roosevelt, as the Republican convention of 1916 approached, hoped to arrange a draft. To his intimates he explained why no one else would do: some had participated in the thievery of 1912 — they could not win Progressive votes; others were too small; still others, including Charles Evans Hughes, the preconvention favorite, not sound on the pressing issues of the day. Roosevelt's agents agreed, but their soundings among Republican delegates revealed how much had to be done. They tried. They organized grass-roots support for Roosevelt, solicited newsworthy signatures to endorse his nomination, transported a serenading throng to Oyster Bay. Once again they had money, and he had it at his disposal, to trade for the prize he had ever sought, the skeleton of the Bull Moose. To save the nation, to defeat Wilson, to elect himself, Roosevelt was at last ready to liquidate his party.

By arrangement the Progressive and Republican conventions met simultaneously, adopted platforms almost identical in their castigation of the Democrats and their emphasis on Americanism and preparedness, and turned to selecting candidates. Restraining a rank and file impatient to nominate Roosevelt, the Progressive powers opened negotiations with the Republicans. Quickly they learned what they had feared: the leaders of the Grand Old Party simply would not nominate its strenuous apostate or any of his fellows. Bargaining could proceed only on Republican terms. In a last futile gesture, Roosevelt urged a common nomination of Henry Cabot Lodge, his oldest friend, whose attitude toward the war canceled out, as far as Roosevelt was concerned, his lifetime of standpattism. But the Republicans, seeking a winner, named the more progressive Hughes, and the Progressives, shouting down a candidate so foreign as was Lodge to their first purpose, nominated Roosevelt. Repulsed by the prospect of a futile canvass, preferring almost anyone to Wilson, assured that Hughes would campaign vigorously, Roosevelt declined his nomination, disbanded his party, and urged its members to return with him to the party of their old allegiance.

Disappointed though he was, Roosevelt stumped hard for Hughes. Without reserve he drew upon all the private and political capital he had left. But many Progressives, dismayed by Roosevelt's turn or by the indifference attending their homecoming, simply sat the election out or supported Wilson. The Democrats, moreover, had capital of their own: the achievements of their Congresses, the President's prestige, their telling slogan — so despised by Roosevelt — "He kept us out of war." By a narrow margin Wilson won.

Roosevelt fumed; Hughes's "overcaution, his legalism, his sluggish coldness of nature, and his sheer inability to grapple with great issues, made him a complete failure." Wilson was a "Byzantine logothete," "exceedingly base," his soul "rotten through and through," "a very timid man" possessing "a merciless vindictiveness and malice." "One large factor in the vote for Wilson," Roosevelt exploded to William Allen White, "was the 'he kept us out of war' cry . . . This is yellow, my friend! plain yellow!" The people "had no ethical feeling . . . ; they weren't concerned with honor or justice or self-respect; they were concerned for the safety of their own carcasses . . . Hughes did not stand for the things for which I stood — that is why he was nominated . . . I was literally the only national leader who dared stand straight on Americanism, preparedness and the performance of international duty . . . I still fail to see anything but degradation in the . . . appeal to the yellow streak . . . Hughes and the Republicans tried to beat skimmed milk with cambric tea; they earned their defeat." So rancorously, as to reassure himself he had to, did the hero pronounce his country unheroic. Larger troubles were to come.

They came with war. Wilson, his patience exhausted, sorrowfully led the country into war in April 1917. Roosevelt immediately endorsed the President's war message and his conscription program; he also immediately requested, as he had long planned, authorization to recruit and lead a volunteer division to the front. This opportunity he wanted as much as he had ever wanted anything. It was refused. For the denial Wilson had cause. He doubted Roosevelt's capacity to command troops in the trench warfare of 1917. He felt that the recruitment and staffing of a volunteer division would interfere with the conscription and training program. Doubtless he also took some satisfaction, possibly had some motivation, in hurting an antagonist. Roosevelt begged the President and Secretary of War to reconsider, pointed out that the French wanted his division, explained how careful were his plans, defended his military competence — in vain. However justified, however spiteful Wilson's denial, it was a cruel blow. Despondent, Roosevelt remained at home, a civilian, and sent his four sons to France. "The big bear," he wrote his eldest son, "was not, down at the bottom of his heart, any too happy at striving to get the . . . little bears where the danger is; elderly bears whose teeth and claws are blunted by age can far better be spared; but (to change from allegory to the first person!) I do not sympathize with the proverb: — 'God keep you from the werewolf and from your heart's desire!' It is best to satisfy the heart's desire; and then abide the fall of the dice of destiny."

For Roosevelt, though his heart's desire had been denied, the

dice fell badly. One son was wounded, another — the youngest
— killed. Disappointment and anguish aged and warped him.
Uninhibited by the responsibility of office, losing his sense of
proportion, yet still ambitious at least for his ideas and his party,
and toward Wilson fiercely vindictive, he let his worst too often
inundate his best. To his credit he remained receptive to new
ideas. Merging some of these with his older thoughts on mutualism, he advocated such bold political departures as compulsory
old-age, sickness and unemployment insurance. For good reason
he deplored the continuing opposition by prominent Democratic
congressmen to war measures, the recurring instances of partisanship and maladministration in the executive's conduct of the war.
But despising Wilson as he did, he could not comprehend that
the conduct of the war, an enormous task, constantly improved.
Nor could he resist exploiting the emotions bred by war.

Roosevelt first contributed to and then capitalized upon war-
time hysteria. Exaggerating the distortions of what he called
Americanism, he asserted in many different ways that opinion
was either white or black, men patriotic or seditious. "He who is
not with us, absolutely and without reserve of any kind," he
wrote, "is against us, and should be treated as an alien enemy
. . . We have room in this country for but one flag . . . We have
room for but one language . . . [We must] crush under our
heel every movement that smacks in the smallest degree of play-
ing the German game." Socialism, pacifism, pornography, free
love, the German language became, in his gospel of blind loyalty,
somehow all one. He revived the noxious proclivity of nativism to
identify the foreign-born and radical. By his standard he damned
conscientious objectors, constitutional Socialist candidates, and
the National Nonpartisan League. He condoned mob action
against labor radicals, pilloried those who strove to protect dissenters, fed the spirit that expressed itself in lynchings, amateur
witch hunts, intolerance of every kind. Roosevelt was not alone
in this. Indeed, at times he ran afoul of government agencies that
behaved his way toward him. But if he was not alone, he was

also not often surpassed in his excursions into hate and his paeans to conformity. The part of him that had always seen the Jacobin in his opponents now ran amuck. And he mixed his hateful talk with his awful cult of purging society by sacrifice in war and his ardent advocacy of compulsory peacetime industrial service for young men and women — an amalgam of conceptions which in another form the world later learned to dread. He disgraced not just his own but his nation's reputation.

If belief, woefully misplaced, actuated Roosevelt, so also did expediency. As early as 1913 he had expressed a calculating interest in "the wild delight" an audience in Boston showed when he denounced the "red flag of anarchy." Seeking an enthusiastic audience, he developed during the war that dismal tactic of recent American demagoguery, the art of seeing red in every opposition. Just as he understood the dangers to America of a triumphant Germany, so did he understand the evil of Bolshevism. He wisely warned his countrymen against them both. But he also confused them both with men he disliked and ideas he rejected, confused them in part — though perhaps not by design — so as to persuade his audience with wild delight to go his way.

His way was partisan, his objective the reëstablishment of Republican rule. Most of his life this had been his goal. He pursued it now with new intensity born of frustration, ire, and dismay at Wilson's attitude toward the impending termination of the war. As the campaign of 1918 approached, Wilson was endeavoring to negotiate an armistice. He had announced his celebrated fourteen points for peace, including his grand plan for the creation of a league of nations. Roosevelt led the Republican chorus of disapproval. German surrender should be unconditional, he urged, dictated to the barking of machine guns, not the chattering of the President's private typewriter. The terms of peace should be severe, he cautioned, the victorious powers — contrary to his interpretation of Wilson's program — permitted to decide without reference to any international body their policies for tariffs, immigration, and armaments. He had "never known," he told a like-minded friend, "a professional internationalist who was worth his salt." "Nationalism," he boasted, "is the keynote of your attitude and mine."

It was also one keynote of the Republican campaign of 1918. Pitched as it was to the sentiments bred by war, it contributed to the party's victory that year. Roosevelt exulted. He had been vindicated, he believed; Wilson, repudiated. And just in time, for the armistice followed close upon the election. Republican control of both houses of Congress would check the President who no longer, Roosevelt informed his French and British friends, spoke for the nation. To them Roosevelt outlined his own plans for peace — handsome reparations for Belgium and France, British and Japanese dominion in former German colonies, some self-determination as Wilson wanted, but instead of a league of nations, an Anglo-American alliance. This was an ordering of the world by victorious powers, the kind of order he had always had in mind. If Wilson's program for world order was perhaps impracticable, Roosevelt's too practically defended an inflexible post-bellum status quo.

At home, working with Republican leaders, Roosevelt had begun to build for 1920. Some of them and some of his old friends hoped that he might then bear the party's standard. He sensed he could not, but he surely would have liked to. He sounded notes reminiscent of his finest hours. "I wish to do everything in my power," he explained to William Allen White, "to make the Republican Party the Party of sane, constructive radicalism," to avoid "merely . . . criticism, delay and reaction," to prepare a liberal platform "satisfactory to conscientious, practical and courageous men . . ." He had warned the Republicans in Congress that they faced "a changed world," that "mere negation and obstruction and attempts to revive the dead past spelled ruin." This was not the sterile normalcy that Warren Harding came to. This was the Roosevelt of his prime writing "I . . . trust

to nothing but our own strength for our own self-defense . . .";
"the only, and the final, test of theory is the service test"; "our
affair is to get our democracy to discipline itself . . ."

But his prime was long past. Grieved by the family toll the
war had taken, rheumatic, ill in age's many ways — though only
sixty, Roosevelt died in the first week of 1919. The immediate
cause of his death was an embolism, the underlying cause the
strenuous life of sixty years. Only hours before he died the Roosevelt of his prime wrote a last note; the professional Republican
politician from New York left a final earnest for Will Hays, the
Republican National Chairman. "Go to Washington for 10 days,"
he scribbled; "see Senate & House; prevent split on domestic
policies."

*

America missed Roosevelt. It missed his spirit. It missed his
fun. Even his critics knew when he died that there was no one
quite like him to take his place. The Republicans missed Roosevelt, too. They missed his resilience, his world-mindedness, his
vitality. Unhappily, in power they pursued too long his last, worst
contributions to their platform; in opposition they persisted in
his last, worst habits. Unhappily, too, this lingering legacy de-
spoiled his memory.

The tragedy of Theodore Roosevelt was that this was bound to
happen. That passionate tension pursuing power never quite
controlled itself. Not all the techniques mastered, not all the expert and moral men summoned to advise, not all the intuition and
compassion, not all the adroitness in negotiation or the measured
sense of pace of change, not all the nice perceptions about social
organization subdued his lust to rule. He let his leadership de-
generate to demagoguery, his patriotism to perfervid chauvinism,
his viable conservatism to a creed akin to fascism. He wrecked
his party, wounded men he had trusted most, deceived the people
who trusted him. All this he did, persuaded that he had to. For
this a knowing chorus can only sorrow.

After all, he understood man's problem. "There is not one among us," Roosevelt wrote the poet Robinson, "in whom a devil does not dwell; at some time, on some point, that devil masters each of us; he who has never failed has not been tempted; but the man who does in the end conquer, who does painfully retrace the steps of his slipping, why he shows that he has been tried in the fire and not found wanting. It is not having been in the Dark House, but having left it, that counts . . ." Before he died he left revolt, that darkest house of politics, his calling. Before he died he admonished his unheeding party to face the future, not the past. And before his devil mastered him he left the record of his Presidency — in spite of all its failings, a splendid record. He left, it is true, frightful examples of intolerance to beware, of conscienceless oppositionism to avoid, of private anxieties to cure. But he also left a model of how to govern, a chart — not accurate, but suggestive — of modern social order, and a vibrant lesson in how to live.

As Roosevelt phrased it for himself, "how very fortunate we have all been . . . we have encountered troubles and at times disaster and we cannot expect to escape a certain grayness in the afternoon of life — for it is not often that life ends in the splendor of a golden sunset." His, to be sure, did not. He took arms against a sea of troubles and by opposing lost too much. Perhaps he can now be forgiven. Surely he can be mourned.

INDEX